OH NO, NOT LOUISE!

by
Louise Holzendorf Burnam

Our confessions are very important. I wrote in my Bible on January 26, 1992:

**JESUS IS LORD OF MY LIFE
NO MATTER WHAT HAPPENS TO ME!
I CAN TAKE IT!
BECAUSE JESUS LIVES BIG IN ME!**

In memory of my faithful sister Joan, who demonstrated unconditional love to me during my recovery.

Table of Contents

Acknowledgements

I am deeply grateful to many special people in my life.

To my loving mother Bernice, for her endless prayers.

To my prayer warrior sisters and brothers:

Betty
Kenneth Mae
Marion
King
Clarence
Maurice
Joan

To all of my nieces, nephews, aunts, uncles, and cousins, thanks for your prayers.

To my husband Jon, who stuck by me for better and for worse.

To my typist Chiresse, for her patience, love and kindness as my sister in Christ and also for demonstrating her professionalism in putting together this book to glorify our Lord.

Most of all to my Savior, Jesus Christ.

Thank You.

LOUISE

VICTORIOUS LOVE

For whosoever is born of God overcometh the world: and this is the victory tht overcometh the world, even our faith.

(1 John 5:4 KJV)

...for every child of God can obey him, defeating sin and evil pleasure by trusting Christ to help him.

(1 John 5:4 TLB)

This book is written on a reading level for primary school children, as well as adults. I feel we need to start at an early age teaching our children the power of prayer.

Introduction

This book tells the story of a young lady who grew up in an unhappy world which she had created for herself. The phrase, "You are your worst enemy", describes me. When I was growing up as a teenager, I thought everyone looked better than I did. My skinny, frail body made me sad. When I received compliments from others, all I could see was a flat-chested, skinny teenager. I was ashamed to put on shorts or bathing suits. My sisters were healthy looking and not ashamed. "Why should they be?" I thought.

My sister Kenneth Mae was one of those high-stepping majorettes. I remember many times observing her getting ready for parades. She would put on a cute little majorette outfit with pretty white boots. Of course, she had one of those well-shaped bodies I longed for. I remember staring at her and hoping one day I would look like her. I was very happy that she was a majorette.

How I longed to have a well-shaped body. I know now, watching too many soap operas made me dislike myself even more. How I longed to look older, and how I longed to look like the young women in those stories. How I longed for the beautiful clothes they wore. I constantly stared into the mirror and imagined how I would look when I grew older. Little did I know, looking young would follow my family and me throughout our careers.

Although at times the weather was very hot and miserable, I would put on two slips or two pairs of pants to fill out my clothes. I was always comparing myself with others.

Because of my self-consciousness, I missed out on a lot of fun growing up. Feeling tired and not having much energy was also part of my life. Being anemic didn't help the situation and later on, I was diagnosed with Lupus. Taking vitamins and eating rare liver was a normal routine for me.

I received salvation many years after marriage. A whole new world opened up to me. My nephew, A. C. Richards, was on fire for the Lord and witnessed to the entire family. Thank God for using him to spread His Word to us.

I now saw myself as a new person, loved by man and most of all by God. Although I continued to long for a mature body, I was finally happy.

I loved my job, I loved my home, I loved my husband, and most of all, I loved Jesus and myself. I was made by God himself! "See! I will not forget you. I have carved you on the palm of my hand." (Isaiah 49:15 King James Version)

By this time I was putting on a little weight, looking and feeling better. I liked to wear suits. Jon and I would shop together and he helped me to choose the best suits for me. Later on that evening I would model them for him.

Now, it's "Oh no, not Louise of all people". I found myself with amputations! My fingers gone! My legs gone! As I write these words the feeling of waking up from a bad dream comes to mind. My God! How I wish it was a dream, but it's not.

When I couldn't breathe on my own and had to ride around with an oxygen tank I would pray, "Oh Jesus, just let me breathe again without this machine." Guess what?

He did! When I had to call for nurses to assist me in the hospital, I would pray, "Oh Jesus, just enable me to walk into the bathroom by myself again." He did! When I had to be pushed around in a wheelchair, I would pray, "Oh Jesus, I can't stand this wheelchair! Just enable me to walk again." He did! I'm walking! When I had to be driven around by relatives to rehab and doctor visits, I would pray, "Oh Jesus, just let me be able to drive my car again!" He did! I'm driving! Oh yes, I am standing and greeting at my church door.

I hope this book will help others to realize how important it is to have a close relationship with Jesus. Without God, I know I wouldn't have wanted to continue to live. I don't care how much love I had from my husband, family, and friends, I know death would have been welcome by me.

He giveth power to the faint; and to them that have no might be increaseth strength. Even the youths shall faint and be weary, and the young men shall utterly fall: But they that wait upon the Lord shall renew their strength; they shall mount up with wings as eagles; they shall run, and not be weary; and they shall walk and not faint.

(Isaiah 40:29-30 KJV)

He gives power to the tired and worn out, and strength to the weak. Even the youths shall be exhausted, and the young men will all give up. But they that wait upon the Lord shall renew their strength. They shall mount up with wings like eagles; they shall run and not be weary, they shall walk and not faint.

(Isaiah 40:29-30 TLB)

First Choice Medical

March 9, 1998

RE: LOUISE BURNAM
   3244 Fireside Drive
   Meadowbrook, FL 32068

To Whom It May Concern:

Ms. Burnam has been a patient of mine for the past 2 years. She has a very interesting medical history. Several years ago, patient had developed upper respiratory infection symptoms, which progressed into fairly significant broncho pneumonia and the patient ended up being hospitalized. At that time, patient developed what is known as adult respiratory distress syndrome. Basically, that is a shutdown of the normal mechanism of the lungs, and patient ended up being placed on a ventilator in order to breathe for her. Patient then went into a coma for a fairly significant amount of time. Adult respiratory distress syndrome is a very serious and usually fatal complication of some respiratory or systemic problem. Unfortunately, probably secondary to the adult respiratory distress syndrome, patient also developed vasculitis. Vasculitis is an internal destruction of the blood vessels to the body and with the deterioration of the blood vessels, obviously the tissues supplied by them are also destroyed. Once again, vasculitis is usually an irreversible process for which there is no permanent treatment and it is usually a fatal sequela as well. When the patient did awake from the coma, the patient had found that both her legs, below the knees, had been amputated and that all of the digits of her two hands had been amputated. These were necessary, secondary to the vasculitis, which had totally destroyed the tissues of the fingers and the legs. For some reason, both the vasculitis and the adult respiratory distress syndrome were totally reversed and treated. The patient woke up with little, if any, permanent sequela, as far as lungs or other major blood vessels to her body. The question can be asked, " Why with a simple respiratory infection, did she develop both the adult respiratory distress syndrome and the secondary vasculitis?" and then the question needs to be further asked, " Why with both the adult respiratory distress syndrome and the vasculitis, did the patient live?"

If you have any further questions or concerns, please don't hesitate to call.

Sincerely,

Barbara L. Cruikshank, M.D.

BC/tt

550-17 Wells Road • Orange Park, FL 32073 • (904) 269-2900 • Fax (904) 269-1140

Chapter One

The Nightmare Begins

I was decorating the walls in my school on December 9, 1994. All of a sudden, my body became very tired. I didn't think this was unusual, because I had worked on other projects between my regular classes before. I stopped working for a while, and laid my head on the desk. I continued working until the end of that day.

I drove home, cooked dinner for my husband, Jon, watched a little TV and went to bed. Around one o'clock that morning I opened my eyes and my chest felt heavy. It felt like a heavy object was pressing down on me. I was also experiencing a little discomfort in breathing. I immediately got up from my bed to put on my clothes and makeup. You see, I always had to look my very best wherever I went around the house and even out to my mailbox. After dressing, I woke Jon up and told him what I was experiencing. I knew I should go immediately to the hospital and he agreed with me.

I went for those once a year doctor check up tests. I took vitamins three times a day, tried to eat healthy foods, and exercised. Yet, here we are heading for the hospital.

We got into our white Corvette, which has been my favorite color since I became born again, and were on our way. The ride to the hospital seemed like a hundred miles to me that very early morning. We lived in Middleburg, Florida which is approximately twenty-five miles from Jacksonville and the hospital. Our beautiful dream home was found there with lovely scenery and most of all wonderful neighbors. I saw our home in a dream one night. I saw beautifully built homes with pretty flowers of all colors, trees molded into beautiful shapes. The sun was shining like a picture-perfect post card, which gave me a peaceful feeling. We were very proud of our home. We finally arrived at the hospital. Jon let me out at the emergency entrance while he parked the car. I walked quickly to the receptionist desk and I remembered talking to a lady and from there on my memory is lost. I don't remember giving my name, but Jon said I did. He said that I was given tests and was diagnosed with pneumonia. He admitted me into the hospital and was thinking that I would probably be there for a few days.

My memory of this time is still lost. The doctor told Jon my lungs were as hard as leather. This really surprised me, because prior to this time I wasn't sick. When my family visited me, Jon said that I was laughing and talking. My doctor wanted to know if I was this way all of the time, because I should have been feeling very sick.

ALL OF A SUDDEN

I started coughing uncontrollably. The coughing was putting too much stress on my body and was affecting my breathing. It was then decided that my body should be shut down. I was placed in ICU (Intensive Care Unit) in a coma on the respiratory machine. Intensive Care Unit; coma; respiratory machine; these are words I have heard of on television, read in books and in newspapers. These words are now a part of my life.

Trust in the Lord with all thine heart; and lean not unto thine own understandings. In all thy ways acknowledge him, and he shall direct thy paths.

(Proverbs 3:5-6 KJV)

If you want favor with both God and man, and reputation for good judgment and common sense, then trust the Lord completely; don't ever trust yourself. In everything you do, put God first, and he will direct you and crown your efforts with success.

(Proverbs 3:5-6 TLB)

Chapter Two

Dreams, Dreams, Dreams

I had several dreams while I was in the coma. My dreams were about a cake sale, a healing, hospital weekend parties, my husband and brother studying my hospital records, taking psychological tests, getting a makeover from my head to my toe and also about my former pastor jumping through a window to see me. I have always wondered what could be going on in a comatose patient's mind. Maybe they were in another world like me, dreaming.

THE HEALING DREAM

I remembered attending a service in a big white church made in the style of a coliseum. A sermon on healing was being preached by a cousin of mine. In real life I do have twin cousins, but neither is a preacher or lawyer; but in this world of dreams they were. They were identical, medium height, wore glasses and were very friendly. I remembered sitting up high in the congregation looking down at my cousin the preacher, who was giving a message on healing. He was telling the people that were sick to believe that they could be healed. They were told to act out their faith. At this time I wasn't conscious of the fact that I couldn't walk; but all of a sudden an inner strength took over my body, and I stood up slowly. I couldn't believe it! I was taking baby steps! I was walking! My cousin saw what was happening and started encouraging me to keep on moving. That huge congregation had all eyes on me. I felt embarrassed but happy.

I then found myself on top of a tall building. Somehow, throughout this dream I had a guilty feeling about my condition. I felt like I was the cause of it. Then I knew why. I was told by my cousins that drugs had been given to me and I fell off of this building. I thought, "I didn't do drugs, how could this be happening?" This part of my healing dream ended with questions in my mind.

THE CAKE SALE DREAM

This next dream doesn't surprise me at all because I love sweets. I can remember fasting from sweets for a month. That first week was the hardest. In my teen years I couldn't eat enough Mr. Goodbars and Baby Ruth candy bars.

My cake sale dream is short, but it is still very clear in my mind. Again, I was in this big, white, beautiful church. There were many, white cakes all over the stage. There were no strawberry cakes, no chocolate cakes, no pound cakes and not even angel food cake, just white icing cakes. I remembered raising my hand to purchase one. It looked so good I couldn't wait to taste it. This dream ends on a sweet note.

WEEKEND PARTIES DREAM

Here is a disturbing, uncomfortable dream. Every weekend the nurses and doctors on my floor would have drug parties on the hospital floor under me. How I knew they were doing drugs, I don't know. The parties were very loud and I felt scared and neglected. I could hear people laughing and talking. I had a feeling my husband was down there. I remember calling out to one of the nurses to go down there and tell Jon I needed him. I can still see Nurse Barbara, a small, petite Indian woman who loved the Lord. My sister Joan and I had many wonderful times talking with her about Jesus. I said to her, "You know my husband, don't you? Please get him for me. I need him."

I could see her looking for him in a room filled with smoke. I guess when you are dreaming in a coma you can see through walls. She came back and said, "I didn't see him." These parties went on and on into the early morning hours. I felt an urge to report this to the administrator of the hospital, but I had no one to help me. A helpless feeling just covered my body. I had this dream several times. Thank God it ended.

MY HOSPITAL RECORDS DREAM

From time to time I would see my husband Jon with a doctor's white coat on. He would have this big black book in his hands. I knew these were my hospital records he was studying. What was strange about this situation was when he completed his task, he didn't come to my room. My room had glass all around it and the curtains would always be open. I could see the entire staff. I would say to myself, "Why doesn't he come to my room?" I felt so neglected. He would always be surrounded by nurses and doctors. He had many discussions with them. I thought, "Maybe he's on staff."

Just like I saw Jon going over my records, my brother King did the same thing. He would be dressed in a suit walking around with this big black book. He also had discussions with the staff. Again, I felt bad and afraid. Why weren't they visiting me? Did I do something wrong? Why am I being treated this way? How I longed for some answers.

TAKING TEST DREAM

I remember taking tests at an Eckerd's store. A tablet was given to me, and I was told to connect dots. There were other patients there taking tests too. I was also given blocks to arrange in order. Sometimes my sisters would be there looking on. I had a feeling they knew the correct order, but couldn't help me. I sensed the therapist wanted my family there for encouragement.

There was a time when my sisters were not with me and I was being observed by a young man. I was working on a test and he made a pass at me. He pressed his face close to mine. Somehow I knew he was married to a beautiful woman. His actions disgusted me and all I could say was, "Why?" I remember having on a trench coat and sadly walking home alone in the dark.

I took these tests many times with my family looking on. I was never told the reasons for the tests but I always had a feeling they were psychological.

THE MAKE-OVER DREAM

I have imagined from time to time how I could make myself look different but was afraid to actually do it, like most women. My wish was granted in this dream.

I found myself in a condominium surrounded by a theme park similar to Disney World. The buildings were beautiful and happy people were walking around with smiles on their faces.

One of the friendly ladies started cutting my hair very short. I remembered remaining calm. This surprised me because I have always preferred long hair. I remembered feeling special and pampered. After she cut my hair, then came the coloring, red! Yes, I did say red. I was beginning to look like a different person. I mean really different! I didn't recognize myself. Where was the face I was used to seeing in the mirror? Next came the facial and body massages. They felt wonderful! Beautiful clothes were chosen for me and of course makeup was applied.

I remembered walking down a long stage feeling gorgeous. Here, I was showing off my new look and my beautiful clothes. I was a model! Yes, I was actually acting out one of my childhood fantasies. I went through this wonderful dream several times. How I wished it was real.

PASTOR WILEY TOMLINSON'S DREAM

The last dream was about my former pastor, Wiley Tomlinson. I remember being placed in a room with very wide windows. I saw nurses opening the windows from the hall.

I now found myself being prepped for surgery. I also saw the urgency in the nurses' faces. I thought, "This is a matter of life and death." Why was I so calm? Could this be the result of my praying family and friends who were really praying in the real world? I can tell you, I was experiencing the peace which passes all understanding.

All of a sudden, Pastor Wiley jumped through the window, staring directly at me. I said to myself, "He is going to pray for me." I had heard many of his sermons on faith and trusting God. His sermons were always uplifting and alive. He could explain God's love in such a way you could feel His presence. Every Sunday service left me with hope and more faith in God, encouragement, appreciation of my family and myself. His sermons were very anointed. I am sure there are many others who would agree with me. God has now blessed me with another pastor, Richard Johnson, and I am still being fed the Word in the same manner. Back to Pastor Wiley, God gave him a vision to bless our city with a Christian radio station. What a blessing this station is to our community! The announcers are all spirit-filled men and women of God. Just turning on the radio in my car or home gives me the assurance that there are friends and believers in Christ behind the voices.

Getting back to my dream, I don't actually remember hearing Pastor Wiley pray for me, but knowing him, I'm sure he did. His associate Pastor, Evangelist Joe Robinson's wife was among the nurses preparing me for surgery. She didn't seem to recognize me, and I became frustrated. I wanted to ask her if she remembered me, but my words, for some reason, couldn't come out.

These dreams were very long. I can only give short versions of each. I do remember staring at a ceiling for many hours. I remember the designs in the ceiling tiles. On top of these titles were funny looking cigar-shaped animals all over the ceiling. My thought at this time was, "Please don't let those things fall on me." It seems as if every time a dream was completed, I went back to staring at the same ceiling. Thank God those cigar-shaped animals didn't fall on me.

It would have been great to have had dreams of God, Jesus and heaven, but I didn't. I know one day I will find out why, and also why all of this had to happen to me.

Dreams I can't go into detail about are a funeral, my sister, Joan, trying to get to me, but being stopped by my husband's friend, me boiling peanuts and being held up in a house and Jon couldn't get to me.

I create the fruit of the lips; peace, peace to him that is far off, and to him that is near, saith the Lord; and I will heal him.

(Isaiah 57:19, KJV)

Peace, peace to them both near and far, for I will heal them all.

(Isaiah 57:19, TLB)

Chapter Three

Waking up From the Coma

Jon said during this time my respiratory status continued to decline. I was in a coma for more than a month when the nursing staff noted my hands and feet were described as "slightly mottled." I developed a combination of falling red blood cell mass and poor peripheral circulation, which led to necrosis of both the upper and lower extremities. Necrosis is death of living tissues.

Then the nightmare really began, Jon was told the doctors wanted to bring me out of the coma to see if my brain and internal organs were being affected, thank God they were not. The next news was not so good. They told Jon because of my infections it was necessary to amputate my fingers and legs. They expressed some urgency in this decision so as to keep complications at a minimum. He said this was a very hard decision to make, but he knew I had to have the operation if I were to live.

Jon had a meeting with my family and told them the situation. They wanted to wait for a miracle, but his mind was already made up. He remembered the urgency in the doctor's eyes. He gave his consent.

I had many born-again family members, friends, and churches praying for me.

Thank God for His prayer warriors.

I was also blessed to have my very own doctor, his family and church praying too. I do remember my sister-in-law, Betty, telling me, "Louise, you don't have to have this done to you." I am told my reply was, "I want to live."

My operation was about three hours. When I finally opened my eyes, I observed my hands all bandaged up. The sight of them reminded me of boxing gloves. I knew my fingers were gone, but it felt as if they were still there. My legs were shorter and it also felt as if they were still part of my body, too. Thank God! I would later discover what a blessing it is to have these whole body feelings. But oh! The terrible pain in my hands and legs, I couldn't pray outward, it was all inside. "Please, God, take this pain away. The Lord is my shepherd, I shall not want." Even though the pain was unbearable, I didn't panic when I saw missing body parts, why? I had a peace I couldn't explain.

My life in the hospital was a nightmare. I didn't feel safe in the environment. The atmosphere was very gloomy. I felt helpless, I felt trapped. My thoughts were, "If there was a fire, I couldn't get up and run. Someone could come into my room and harm me." These and other scary thoughts came to my mind over and over. I didn't think of the scripture, (II Tim 1:7, King James Version) "God has not given me a spirit of fear; but of power, love, and a sound mind." I would call out to God, "Please take away the pain." The medication wasn't helping me. My doctor tried his very best to make me comfortable.

The nurses and assistants were very slow in answering my calls. I would call out to God and say, "Please,

God, don't let me have to use the bed pan for the rest of my life." I couldn't stand it. I felt embarrassed and humiliated when help did come.

I knew Jesus loved me. I was born again and had experienced His healing power from Lupus and arthritis. I always had hope and faith, but why was this happening to me now? Before this happened just about every day I would thank God and give Him praise. I told people about Jesus, and even purchased mini Bibles to pass out. I went for those once a year doctor checkups, took vitamins three times a day, tried to eat healthy foods and was into exercising. I had a good husband, a beautiful home, and was happy with my job. Even though my husband at this time was not a Christian, we found happiness in other areas. Now, my whole world had changed. What about Jon? I knew he loved me but could he accept me like this? He always told me I looked good in any outfit I put on. I thought, "How will I look now without fingers and legs? Will I ever drive the Vette again?"

Jon stayed many nights with me in that dreadful room filled with pain, pain, pain. I would call for him all during the night. He brought his clothes and went from the hospital to work. When he arrived to work every morning he would make calls to my mother and his mother and kept them informed on my condition. My mother later on told me how much those calls really meant to her. The family tried to keep her away from the hospital as much as possible.

I would shake with pain and fear when the nurses attempted to change the dressings on my legs. Let me say right here; God made me with legs and as far as I am concerned, what's left of my legs are still legs, not stumps. How I despised that word. It's so demeaning and inhumane. I decided from day one no one, not even the doctors and therapists, would use that word when referring to my body.

As I stated before, I would shake with fear and pain when the dressing on my legs needed changing. My wonderful husband would be there to comfort me and hold my legs still. You see, they were raw. The Lord is my shepherd I shall not want would come to mind. I knew God would have to heal these two pieces of raw flesh, if I were to walk again. How I wish someone had taken pictures of them then, because after many prayers, they were healed.

I could see the doubt in the nurses' eyes when they saw my legs. Sometimes when I observed my legs doubt would try to enter my mind. I couldn't get the words out of my mouth but the Psalm (23:1 King James Version) "The Lord is my shepherd, I shall not want" was on my mind.

Every time a new shift would come on in spite of the fear of pain, I made sure to tell the head nurses, "Don't forget to change my bandages and wet my legs down with saline." You see, these were the doctor's orders. He said this had to be done on time. I found out that all nurses and doctors do not perform equally. I mean some are more professional and caring than others. Even though I suffered with unbearable pain in my body, I learned early that I had to look out for myself. Many people who work in hospitals shouldn't be there.

One morning when Jon and the family weren't around I experienced my body being placed in a sling and lifted up from my bed. I was also having trouble breathing. I moaned softly and said to the nurse and aide, "I can't breathe." They paid no attention to me and then I saw what they were doing; making up my bed. Why they had to put me in this sling, I don't know. I do know this: they didn't care about my feelings, being comforted or showing compassion didn't exist, the pain was unbearable and I felt as if I was dying and wouldn't make it through the day. Why, why, why, did I have to suffer so much in the hands of people in a hospital?

But the salvation of the righteous is of the Lord;
he is their strength in the time of trouble.

(Psalm 37:39, KJV)

The Lord saves the Godly! He is their salvation
and their refuge when trouble comes.

(Psalm 37:39, TLB)

Chapter Four

My Husband's Illness

After all I had to deal with every day, Jon got sick. Because my hands were bandaged up, I had to have everything done for me, face washing, brushing teeth, dressing and feedings. Of course, Jon tried to do it all when he was there. He would tell the nurses they could leave. I was glad because he took his time and had so much patience with me.

Jon wasn't eating properly and wasn't getting enough rest. He didn't have an appetite and was sleeping in a chair next to my bed. Because of his dedication to me, he began experiencing fluttering of the heart. I was always concerned about him not getting enough sleep and not eating. This also made me feel very guilty. I knew my illness was taking too much out of him. He had lost a lot of weight too. I told Jon not to leave the hospital, and to go straight to the emergency area. With a little encouragement from Nurse Brenda, he did. Brenda was an exceptional old fashioned nurse who cared for her patients. I was so happy when the time came for her shift. Thank God for Nurse Brenda.

The next thing I knew Jon was being kept for observations. Can you believe it? Jon was in the hospital too! The doctors wanted to keep him for forty-eight hours. Needless to say, this was a very difficult time for me. I could only say, "The Lord is my shepherd; I shall not want." The pain in my hands and legs seemed to get worse. I was constantly experiencing nausea; in fact, it was always with me, like the pain. To top it all off, I had a raw skin graft on my thigh. My thoughts were, "My God, please take away the pain."

All kinds of thoughts were going through my mind. "What's going to happen to Jon? How will I get along without him? Who's going to hold my legs and comfort me while the nurses change my bandages? "JESUS HELP!" I would ask the nurses to call emergency and find out Jon's condition. Here again the feeling of helplessness and fear engulfed my painful body. When will this nightmare end?

I remember that very day in college when Jon walked up to me while I was sitting on a wall in front of my school. He met three of my qualifications right away: a part in his hair, a neat appearance, and most of all he was very smart and intelligent. I later found out, to my surprise, that he had a good outlook on life and a happy spirit. God put him in my life at the right time. It was a time when I was suffering with Lupus. I didn't know I had the disease, in fact, I hadn't even heard of it. Jon's uplifting spirit was medicine to my bones. God knew Jon would eventually become knowledgeable about vitamins and eating healthy. He knew Jon would see the importance of us living a healthy lifestyle. He knew that he would provide me with the vitamins I needed to help me endure what was to come. God also knew whom I would need during this difficult period in my life. He also knew I would be a good influence in his life too. How I wish Jon could have been spared from this nightmare.

Jon was released after two days of tests and observations. When he walked into my room, I felt so much love for him. He had lost so much weight. I knew it was time for him to sleep at home. Fear struck me again. The thought of not having him next to my bed was terrible. I knew these thoughts were very selfish of me; after all he had other things to take care of, such as our home. Most of all he had a job to go to every day. My hospital ordeal was beginning to get the best of him. Thank You, God, for Jon.

My little children, let us not love in word, neither in tongue; but in deed and in truth.

(1 John 3:18, KJV)

Little children, let us stop just saying we love people; let us really love them, and show it by our actions.

(1 John 3:18, TLB)

Chapter Five

My Family

My family was very dedicated to me too. Thank God for my mother's prayers. Thank God for loving sisters who took care of my needs during the day when Jon was at work. They knew how much I took pride in the way I looked. My sister Joan, who is now in heaven, kept my hair in a beautiful pony tail, brought me beautiful night-gowns and most of all she would lay hands on my raw legs. I could count on her walking into my room every evening, rain or shine. She came in like an angel with a smile on her face. I told her she didn't have to come every day. She also was an elementary teacher, and I knew about those not so good days. Like my husband, she wouldn't even consider missing one day. I love her and miss her so much. Thank God she was saved and is now with Jesus in glory. Thank God I will see her again.

I thank God for my other prayer warrior family members. Sisters: Betty, Kenneth Mae, and Marion. My brothers: Maurice, Clarence, and King. My nieces: Debbie, Cynthia, Monique, Michelle, and Melissa. My nephews: A. C. Richards, Maurice, Todd, and Kent. My mother-in-law: Rose and her family. Most of all my mother: Bernice and many more aunts, uncles, nieces, nephews, and relatives.

We have always been a very close-knit family. Celebrating holidays and birthdays was a welcome routine for all of us. We sang songs, talked about Jesus, danced to praise music and watched the children play.

Even though I didn't have any children of my own, I felt like they were all mine. I love them so much and have started praying for their future wives and husbands. Besides being family members we were friends to each other. Agape love surrounded us. I thank God for saving us.

I thank God for the boldness He placed in my nephew A. C. Richards for sharing the love of Jesus to us. Thank God for his obedience in sharing God's plan of salvation. Sometimes sharing the Gospel with family isn't easy.

Peace I leave with you, my peace I give unto you: Not as the world giveth, give I unto you. Let not your heart be troubled, neither let it be afraid.
(John 14:27, KJV)

I am leaving you with a gift - peace of mind and heart! And the peace I give isn't fragile like the peace the world gives. So don't be troubled or afraid.
(John 14:27, TLB)

Chapter Six

The Male Nurses and Aides

Do you know that there is no such thing as privacy in a hospital? Do you know that hospitals have many male nurses and male aides? Do you know that strangers can walk into your room without being escorted by your nurse or doctor? I found out this is the hospital environment.

Specialists would come into my room and examine me without being escorted by nurses. Some of them wore name tags, others did not. I knew these were supposed to be professional people, but to me they were strangers. I guess this disturbed me more because I didn't have any legs. I constantly felt vulnerable.

Male aides and male nurses are another part of the hospital's environment which made me feel uncomfortable. Sometimes they answered my calls for the bed pan. I would ask for something else, like water. I would say to myself, "No way am I going to let one of them assist me in my personal needs." What are the other female patients doing? Am I the only one feeling this way?"

I decided to tell the head nurse on each shift that I didn't want males taking care of my personal needs. They would smile and say, "OK." My request was honored, but often I had to remind them. I believe there are females out there right now, not speaking up for themselves, thinking they have to accept this. I am saying if you find yourself in a situation like this, speak up! These young men were very friendly and helpful in many other ways.

I also have to say that the majority of these young male nurses I came in contact with were homosexuals. We love the homosexual and hate their lifestyle.

Father, I pray for them right now. Touch their hearts and remove the scales from their eyes. Let them SEE Jesus. Thank You Jesus!

I can do all things through Christ which strengtheneth me.
(Philippians 4:13, KJV)

For I can do everything God asks me to with the help of Christ who gives me strength and power.
(Philippians 4:13, TLB)

Chapter Seven

Hospital Therapy

As my body became stronger, my doctor wanted me to start therapy as soon as possible. To tell you the truth, I didn't know therapy was available in that hospital. I also didn't feel like I was ready for therapy because my body was so weak, and oh yes, the pain was always there. I weighed about ninety pounds. Jon tried to fatten me up by bringing dinners, donuts, pot pies, and candy. I could have really enjoyed these foods but the nausea was always there.

Therapy in the hospital was another nightmare. Experiencing constant pain in my hands and legs brought me to tears many times. The orderlies would come for me every morning after breakfast. Most of them didn't show me any compassion; I was just a job to them. However, I do remember one young man talking to me about his love for Jesus. With the exception of this young man, I didn't like how they transferred me from my bed to the wheelchair. I wasn't able to cover my body properly, you know how hospital gowns fit, and of course no nurses would accompany them. I had to just close my eyes and take it. To make things worse, they would push my wheelchair down the halls so fast it would really upset and frighten me. I just knew one day we would run into someone or something. They also seemed to get a kick out of turning the corners real fast. Thank God we never had an accident.

As I said before, my body was very weak and in terrible pain, which made therapy very unpleasant. On this floor, the physical therapist was a male. This man reminded me of a drill sergeant. He demonstrated to me how to transfer from the wheelchair to the bed. Of course it sounded and looked so easy when he did it. By no means was it easy. Don't tell this to the drill sergeant! "It was simple," he said, "Bend and reach for the bed." Hey! He has all of his fingers, and most of all his legs! It was easy for him! With my body aching with pain, I tried to bend and reach for the cot and almost fell, and you know what? I really don't feel like the drill sergeant would have stopped me from falling. After three meetings with me, I guess he finally realized I wasn't ready for him. Boy was I glad!

My next therapy was the whirlpool. The whirlpool floor was very gloomy. As if that wasn't enough, there was bickering between the therapists. One young lady was constantly on the phone arguing with a relative. I could hear her whole conversation. The other therapist would wait impatiently for her assistance. I was embarrassed for her. When she finally came, she was fussing and carrying on unprofessionally. I really didn't want her messing with my legs.

I couldn't sit inside of the whirlpool because of the skin graft on my thigh. This meant I had to sit up high on a chair with my legs extended into the water. It felt as if I could fall in the water at anytime. Then came more torture, after the whirlpool, the therapist had to prep my legs. This meant scraping off all of the bad tissue. Yes, more fear, pain and disgust with the staff. I thought the pain would never end. I was so weak. All I could say was Jesus, Jesus, and Jesus.

Then came the waiting for the orderly to take me back to my room. I usually had to sit and wait to be returned to my room for up to forty minutes. When he finally got to me, his face was stern and on occasion joked with another co-worker about a new female on the job. Oh how I hated this time and here again, I felt so helpless. Sometimes I wanted to yell, "Hey everybody I wasn't always like this! I use to have fingers and legs like you! I know how it feels to have fingers and legs! See, look at my pictures!" I still feel like yelling this out at times; that's why I now carry a picture of myself of how I used to look in my wallet everywhere I go.

I also had therapy for my hands. This therapist was very caring and professional. She started the therapy in my room. I liked that. I got to stay in my room! Thank God. Therapy consisted of pulling stretching devices to make my hands strong. I thank God for the two partial thumbs on both hands. I shudder to think of how I would have had to adjust with no grip at all. I try to remember to give thanks for them everyday. I also thank God for giving man the knowledge for making prosthetics. Thank God for my man-made legs.

Put on the whole armour of God, that ye may be able to stand against the wiles of the devil. For we wrestle not against flesh and blood, but against principalities, against powers, against rulers of the darkness of this world, against spiritual wickedness in high places.
(Ephesians 6:11-12, KJV)

Put on all of God's armor so that you will be able to stand safe against all strategies and tricks of Satan. For we are not fighting against people made of flesh and blood, but against persons without bodies-the evil rulers of the unseen world; and against huge numbers of wicked spirits in the world.
(Ephesians 6:11-12,TLB)

Chapter Eight

The Evil Spirit

I used to think evil spirits were just bad thoughts or people misbehaving. I was brought up in the Methodist and Lutheran Church and wasn't taught about a real devil out there influencing lives. I never heard of Ephesians 6:11-12, Put on the whole armour of God, that ye may be able to stand against the wiles of the devil. For we wrestle not against flesh and blood, but against principalities, against powers, against the rulers of the darkness of this world, against spiritual wickedness in high places.

When I became born again, I was taught the promises of God and how to stand on them. I was taught to quote scriptures pertaining to whatever needs I might have. I would lay hands on my body and thank God for healing me from my head to toe, even before my body was stricken.

Now, very early one morning in my hospital room, I opened my eyes and what did I see standing in front of me? Well, I can tell you one thing, it wasn't an angel. Maybe this is the reason why I didn't feel safe in that room. I remember telling the night nurse, "Please leave the door open. I want to see the light." I saw a figure of a man dressed in black leaning next to a cross on the wall. That cross was one bright spot in that room. His eyes were glassy and they moved from side to side. He looked very evil. I couldn't see his feet! His presence did not scare me. I was at peace. I didn't quote scriptures, but I just stared at him eye to eye and then he was gone. Yes, I know who tried to kill me. Jesus was with me and still is, Hallelujah. I know someone might say, "She was dreaming" I know I wasn't because I remember opening my eyes.

My prayer was always, "God please take the pain away. Please let me walk again. I feel so helpless, God. I know You love me."

Because the image of this evil spirit is so clear in my mind today, I've had thoughts of making a drawing of it; then again, I just want to erase it from my mind.

Dearly beloved, avenge not yourselves but rather give place unto wrath: for it is written, vengeance is mine; I will repay, saith the Lord.
(Romans 12:19, KJV)

Dear friends, never avenge yourselves. Leave that to God, for he has said that he will repay those who deserve it.
(Romans 12:19, TLB)

Chapter Nine

The Uncaring Surgeon

Life continued to be very scary and painful for me in the hospital. I remember very clearly the doctor who came into my room to pull the stitches out of my legs. They were really staples instead of thread. I guess this procedure is faster for doctors. I wasn't informed that he was coming, and to make the situation worse, I wasn't given medication for the pain I had to endure. He didn't show me any compassion. I guess in his eyes I was just another patient with a number. In fact, I felt that way a lot, "just a number." Oh yes, he did ask me what nationality I was. The first words to come out of my mouth were German. Well, my maiden name is Holzendorf. I know there is some German blood in me, including Indian, Chinese, and Caucasian. He said, "You don't look German." I should have said, "Well, what do I look like?" I guess I still had some humor left in me. By this time, a nurse entered my room and stood beside the bed. This doctor started pulling out the staples from my legs and was hurting me so much. I cried, moaned and became angry. The nurse didn't even comfort me. She just stood there like a statue. At one point I yelled, "You are hurting me!" My moans and sobs didn't do any good. The more I yelled, the more he pulled. He had no compassion! After putting up quite a fuss, he finally left and I learned later he had left some staples in my legs. My mind was made up; should he return I wasn't going to let him touch me again.

Later on that night the head nurse told me she had heard what happened earlier to me with the doctor. I guess the nurse who assisted him reported my continuing nightmare. No thanks to her.

That doctor did return within a few days and I was ready for him. Before he could get to my bed, I said, "I'm afraid of you! You hurt me!" He turned around and I never saw him again. I knew the staples had to come out, but I tried not to think about it. Finally, a nurse took out the remaining staples and I was given medication prior to the procedure. As I think back on this incident, I should have told my husband to report this doctor to the top administrator, but here again, we are at the mercy of these people when we are in the hospital, and don't want to cause trouble. My thinking was limited to surviving through another day and night. I thought, "Is this really a hospital? Am I in the "Twilight Zone?"

Psalm 23, the Lord is my shepherd I shall not want... came to my mind over and over. These words gave me comfort and strength.

Thou wilt keep him in perfect peace, whose mind is stayed on thee because he trusteth in thee. Trust in the Lord for ever: for the Lord Jehovah is everlasting strength:
(Isaiah 26:3-4, KJV)

He will keep in perfect peace all those who trust in him, whose thoughts turn often to the Lord. Trust in the Lord God always, for in the Lord Jehovah is your everlasting strength.
(Isaiah 26:3-4, TLB)

Chapter Ten

The Chainsaw

I've often heard of people having to get skin grafts after an injury or accident; now it was my turn. My doctor said it was necessary for me to have a skin graft on one of my legs. I can only describe both of my legs as looking like pieces of raw meat; one was a little worse than the other and this was the leg that needed new skin. I was nervous over the thought of having to go through another operation. The thought of having to suffer with more pain made me very uncomfortable. A sedative could have helped.

Jon couldn't be with me on the day of my operation but my sister Marion was with me before going to surgery. She gave me a lot of support just being by my side. I later found out she had gotten a speeding ticket trying to get to me. Thank God for sisters like Betty, Kenneth Mae, and Joan, too.

I didn't think the skin graft helped my leg, it was still very raw. Skin was removed from my right thigh and the surgeon placed a cast on it. I experience pain and, of course, soreness. I am reminded every day of this operation because it left an ugly mark on my body. Sometimes I picture the surgeon taking the scalpel and scraping the skin off of my thigh. He said the mark will always be there, but you know me by now; I believe it will be gone one day.

I had no idea when the cast would be removed; I knew the time was getting close. My doctor walked in one day and announced that he was going to remove the cast. I thought he was going to unwrap it by hand. What did I know; this was a first for me. All of a sudden he pulls out this instrument that looks like and, oh yes, sounded like a chain saw. I do remember a nurse holding me down because I was so frightened. Boy could I have used a sedative then. I said to him, "Are you sure you are not going to saw my flesh?" He tried to reassure me, but no words could help me now. He drilled and drilled down into the cast. The noise made the whole ordeal worse. I couldn't take my eyes off of the drill. He drilled for about seven minutes. It felt like an hour. I was so relieved when it was all over. I now had two raw legs and one raw thigh. My, oh my, what's next? Oh yes, now I am experiencing burning pain on five parts of my body. I could turn only on one side.

My thigh healed in two months. I feel for children having to go through the chainsaw ordeal. A sedative could have helped a little, I do mean a little.

Fear thou not; for I am with thee; be not dismayed; for I am thou God: I will strengthen thee; yea, I will help thee; yea I will uphold thee with the right hand of my righteousness.

(Isaiah 41:10, KJV)

Fear not, for I am with you. Do not be dismayed. I am your God. I will strenghten you; I will help you; I will up hold you with my victorious right hand.

(Isaiah 41:10, TLB)

Chapter Eleven

The Blood Diggers

For as long as I can remember, nurses always had a difficult time drawing blood from my veins. They are small and hidden very well under my skin. I am told most women have this problem. The hospital blood diggers, as I call them, also had problems getting blood from my arms. They came into my room early in the morning around 4 a.m. for blood. This time was very scary because the blood diggers would enter my room stone-faced, without a nurse accompanying them. I would always think, "Why are they not friendly? Isn't this a hospital?" These unpleasant males and females would wake me up and tell me they had to fill up two or three tubes of blood. I was still in constant pain and when I finally got to sleep, it was a blessing. But now I was being disturbed from my sleep to endure more pain! I thought, "Oh God how much more pain can I take? These blood diggers dug and dug into my skin until the tubes were all filled. That's why today my arms still carry the unsightly marks of scar tissue. I got so tired of giving blood until one morning I refused the blood diggers.

When my doctor came in that morning I told him what was going on and how it was impossible for me to get back to sleep, even though I had been given a sleeping pill. It was always very easy to talk to this doctor because I knew he really cared about me as a patient. I wasn't just another number. Most of all he was a Christian and I could see the love of Jesus in him. I was truly blessed. He saw to it that no blood was drawn before 6:00 a.m. This made life a little better for me, and it wasn't quite as scary.

For I will restore health unto thee, and I will heal thee of thy wounds, saith the Lord...
(Jeremiah 30:17, KJV)

I will give you back your health again and heal your wounds.
(Jeremiah 30:17, TLB)

Chapter Twelve

On My Way to Rehabilitation

My body was getting stronger and my appetite was better. My doctor said it was time for me to move on to a rehabilitation hospital. The thought of leaving the hospital I hated now frightened me. Can you imagine that? I had been there for so long and even made a few good friends. When you stay in a hospital over a long period of time, there are nurses you prefer attending to your needs more than others. Nurse Brenda on the night shift, yes, I did say night shift, which is the worse shift of all, insisted on giving me a back rub every night. She was very attractive with long dark hair. She spoke encouraging words to me and always had a beautiful smile. She tried to make me as comfortable as possible.

Now let me tell you about my experience with the night shift. The night shift staff was even slower in answering my calls than the day shift. I heard from my room loud conversations concerning the workers' personal lives. I heard loud joking, kidding and laughing throughout the night. This environment added to my uneasiness in that room.

When Jon left after his visits, I dreaded my nights because I knew the events would be repeated and knew what was in store for me.

I remember asking my doctor, "Can this rehabilitation hospital take care of my needs"? He said that they could take care of me better than this hospital. He also said that his mother had gone to this facility and her results were wonderful.

After a few weeks I was accepted into this hospital. Most of the staff were very friendly and caring. I was taught how to dress myself in bed, feed myself again and also how to put on makeup, which was very, very important to me. God was truly with me in surgery when he left two partial thumbs on my hands. What, oh what, would I do without a grip? My below-the-knee amputations are a blessing too. I would learn later on that by having below the knee amputations I could learn to walk quicker with prosthesis.

Therapy was every day, very tiresome, and painful. My body clock was still waking me up on time every morning. I was used to getting up early for my drive to work. This was also good because I wanted to be dressed, have my face washed and teeth brushed before my doctor made his early rounds. I was angered by the fact that I had to ask for my face cloth and toothbrush. Maybe they didn't have many patients who couldn't get out of the bed, I don't know. One nurse would come into my room quickly at 7:00 a.m. on the dot to take my temperature and blood pressure. Another one would come in quickly to give medication for pain and my breakfast. By this time I could feed myself, but I couldn't open the milk cartons and juice containers. I had to ask for help before the nurse got away. You see, during this time they moved fast. I mean very fast. They had other patients to get ready for therapy too. Most of the patients were old, weak, and very slow.

My doctor would come in around 8:00 a.m. to check on my progress and needs. He was an excellent doctor. I remember him giving me a valentine card his daughter made for his patients. I had to be in my wheelchair about 8:50 because therapy was at 9:00 a.m. Yes, I finally learned how to transfer from the bed to the wheelchair with some careful assistance.

Not having legs embarrassed me. I made sure that my body from the waist down was covered before I went anywhere in the wheelchair. The hospital aide would come for other patients and me on the floor. We would be lined up like cattle in the elevator and on our way to the first floor. This made me feel very bad. Little old women and men would look at me with pity in their eyes. I could feel them wondering, "What happened to her? Poor thing." I smiled and said something encouraging, "It's a beautiful day, isn't it?" I knew who I was in Christ then and I know Jesus still has plans for me.

This therapy floor was a world of a difference compared to the other hospital rehabilitation. The room was bright and cheerful, and most of all the therapists were excellent! I couldn't believe it! They were also caring and compassionate! I was always in pain but I still did the exercises. I was motivated. When the physical therapist was finished with me, the next thing I knew the occupational therapist had come for me. When she was finished with me she rolled me over to a Dow group. We sat in a big circle and did exercises with the stick. I enjoyed this group but was very embarrassed sitting in the circle without legs and yes, the stares didn't help at all.

My sister Joan, who is now rejoicing with the Lord in heaven, shopped for my therapy clothes and had my outfits ready for me every morning. She would visit me every evening after a long day in school with her students. Joan always saw to it that my hair was well groomed. She would fix my hair into a beautiful ponytail every evening. Again, I told her she didn't have to come every evening but, like my husband, they still came. Joan also prayed every visit for my legs to heal. One leg was still raw. I didn't see much hope for my legs in the nurse's eyes, but guess what? They finally healed! God is so good!

One morning, to my surprise, in walked a psychiatrist. I guess because of my condition, my doctor felt I might need some counseling. I must say an ordinary person, who went through what I did, would definitely need the service. You see, I am different; I had and still have a personal relationship with Jesus Christ. I had and still have a husband and family who care for me. I have peace within, peace which amazes me sometimes.

The first time this young lady came to my room, I honestly felt offended by her presence. I knew I didn't need her service. She needed what I had and still have. Of course like all psychiatrists she wanted me to pour my heart out to her, but that didn't happen. I told her I got my strength from Jesus and that he would help me through this difficult time in my life. She tried to make me feel as if what I was saying was nonsense. I could sense her thinking, "How could you possibly be saying this? Look at you." I wanted her to know I wasn't suicidal. I had peace in my heart. She tried over and over to get me to feel sorry for myself, but her persistence couldn't move me. She became annoyed and, with a phony little smile, was out the door!

She came back the following week trying again to make me feel sorry for myself. It still didn't work. This time she didn't stay as long as our first visit. She left the same way she did the first time with a phony smile and out the door. I said to myself, "I'm going to have to take charge of this situation. She is annoying me."

Every morning the head nurse would come into my room with a pleasant smile and ask how I was doing, and if I needed anything. On one of her visits I told her I did not need the services of the psychiatrist. Thanks, but no thanks. She smiled and said OK. She got the message. I never saw the psychiatrist again. Now believe me, I'm not putting down psychiatrists. I know there are many people out there in need of their services. I'm just one of the exceptions. Thank God!

I was in this hospital a little over two months.

Casting all your care upon him; for he careth for you.

(1 Peter 5:7, KLV)

Let him have all your worries and cares, for he is always thinking about you and watching everything that concerns you.

(1 Peter 5:7, TLB)

Chapter Thirteen

Weekend Home Visits

I was allowed two weekend home visits during my stay in rehab. I must say two very painful visits. All kinds of negative thoughts entered my mind when I thought about going home. Thoughts like, "You can't walk, you can't cook, and you can't do anything. All you can do is to sit in that wheelchair! Why do you want to go home?" Then I said to myself, "Get a hold of yourself! It's going to be OK. You can do it!"

Jon seemed to be calm and collected when it was time for me to go on my first weekend visit. He came for me around 11:00 a.m. on a Saturday morning. I had my clothes on and was ready to go. He pushed me down to the nurse's station and signed me out. I was going to see my home again! I was so excited! Negative thoughts were now far from my mind. We took the elevator down to the first floor where our car was parked. I transferred from my wheelchair into the car seat, so far so good. When Jon pulled away from the building, I immediately sensed something was wrong. I thought, "I know what's wrong. I can't put on brakes! I have no feet even though all feeling of having my feet were still there!" You see, my husband's favorite sport is car racing; you know what that means; yes, he drives fast! I was always putting on brakes on my side of the car. I'm sure a lot of wives can identify with this.

My body felt so strange in the car without feet. A terrible feeling came over me. "Oh God, Oh God, help me! Please make these feelings go away! I need my legs! Help me Jesus, help me!"

The feeling became more unbearable as we got closer to home. Jon turned in to a grocery store parking lot and said that he had to get a few items. I watched people walk in and out of the store, paying attention particularly to their legs. I'm saying to myself, "My, oh my, I remember when I could walk and run like that." Then I saw a familiar face. I saw my sister Marion. I yelled, "Marion! Marion"! I was so happy to see her. We talked for a little while and Jon returned. We said good-bye and were on our way home again. Now, the bad feeling returns. Little did I know that there would be a bigger challenge ahead of me.

The first challenge was just trying to get my wheelchair inside the house. We found out that the doors in our home were not wide enough for my wheelchair. Jon had to push and try to maneuver my chair through the narrow entrance. I finally made it through. Home, home, home, for a few moments. I was happy. Jon sat me on the sofa, oh, oh, here we go again, "I need my legs!" I remember seeing legs in front of me when I sat on my sofa, but not now. We talked and watched TV. I felt so guilty when he had to do everything such as cooking, cleaning, and assisting me.

Now, here comes the second challenge, the bathroom. I thought trying to get inside the house was bad, little did I know the door entrances inside of the house were worse. I prayed, "Please let me get this chair into my bathroom, Jon is trying so hard." He pushed and pushed until we finally made it through. We went through this scene many times. I felt so bad for the trouble I was causing, and so much love for Jon. His patience and loving care just tore me up inside. He didn't deserve a wife like this and he didn't marry me like this. "Help me, dear God! Help me!" I was so embarrassed for not having legs. I thought, "How could he ever accept me this way? He's not even a Christian!"

Sleeping again in my own bed was wonderful. I thought, "If I could only take this bed back with me. If only I didn't have to go back." If only, if only, if only... The reality was that I had to get stronger, I wasn't ready for home at this time, but I knew the time would come.

My therapy continued and my body became stronger and stronger. I knew my days at the rehabilitation center would soon be over. No more waking up at 6:30 every morning trying to get ready for my 7:00 a.m. doctor visit. NO MORE calling for assistance, NO MORE being rounded up like cattle on the elevator, NO MORE patient stares, waiting for my sister Joan and Jon to walk into my room. No more, no more, no more, Praise God!

The Lord will perfect that which concerneth me: Thy mercy, O Lord, endureth forever; forsake not the works of thine own hands.
(Psalm 138:8, KJV)

The Lord will work out his plans for my life – for your lovingkindness, Lord, continues forever. Don't abandon me – for you made me.
(Psalm 138:8, TLB)

Take therefore no thought, for the morrow. For the morrow shall take thought for the things of itself.
(Matthew 6:34, KJV)

So don't be anxious about tomorrow. God will take care of your tomorrow too. Live one day at a time.

(Matthew 6:34, TLB)

Chapter Fourteen

Home Again for Good

Praise the Lord! I'm home again! I told my husband and my family that I wanted to take care of myself, now that I was home. Jon continued taking care of me and I told my mother that I would call her when I needed her help. She, being a loving and caring person, was very concerned. Jon could accept this, but it was hard for her.

I knew Jesus would give me the strength needed to take care of myself. Can you imagine being in a wheelchair, without legs and fingers, believing you could do everything for yourself? I would say this is what I call a very strong faith in God. The scripture, "I can do all things through Christ which strengthens me," Philippians 4:13 (King James Version) comes to my mind.

One morning, home alone, a wasp found its way into my living room. While riding around in my wheelchair doing chores, all of a sudden it came right up to my face, and without thinking, I hit at it with a piece of paper. Before I knew it my body had fallen to the floor! What an awful feeling. Here I am on the floor, with no one around, and most of all without legs. I prayed and ask God to help me get back in the chair. Just as quick as I had fallen to the floor, somehow I was back in my chair. This was the first time I was glad to be back in that chair again.

Another time while dusting furniture in my bedroom, a dresser with a statue on top of it fell on me. It pinned me down on my bed. I prayed, "Please God, help me get this dresser off of me!" God gave me the strength to push it back up, and guess what! The statue fell to the side of my face and didn't touch me. Hallelujah! God is so good.

I started doing a little cooking, ironing, and sweeping from my wheelchair. Can you believe it? I even picked up a needle and did some sewing. Remember, I'm working without fingers. I prepared dinner by cutting up vegetables and making salads. Jon made sure all items were within my reach. He did all of the stove cooking. Jon cooked many meals for us before I was able to take over.

After a few appointments with Todd, my prosthetics provider, I received my new legs. Now, it was time for therapy again. Oh no, not again! How else was I going to learn to walk on my beautiful legs?

I enrolled in a rehabilitation facility as an outpatient, not too far from my home. Jon made sure I was there on time every evening after his work. He had so much patience with me. This was truly agape love.

This center was very small compared to the other rehabilitation center. The therapists there were super. The only problem I had with this facility was that my therapist, Stan, would have me practice walking on the sidewalk, outside of the building, on a very busy street. Needless to say, I didn't like the attention from the people in their cars. I was still a little weak and still had to continue my strengthening exercises. You know by now that I have much faith, but sometimes when I looked at my prosthesis a little doubt would come to mind. "How in the world will I be able to walk on these man-made legs?" From the wheelchair to the walker and to a cane, I learned to walk. The more I tried the easier it got. I took baby steps to adult steps. "Hey! I can walk! I will never take these legs off!" I quickly found out they would have to eventually come off. I even tried sleeping in them. Therapy continued for about three months. My physical therapist, Stan, had much patience and care for me.

O give thanks to the Lord; for he is good: for his mercy endureth for ever.

(Psalm 136:1, KJV)

Oh, give thanks to the Lord for he is good; his loving-kindness continues forever.

(Psalm 136:1, TLB)

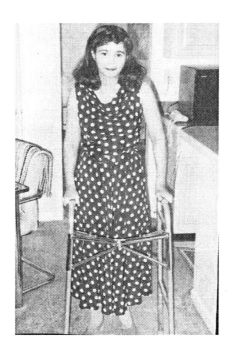

Chapter Fifteen

Driving Rehabilitation

Before my amputations I gave thanks to God for giving me the opportunity to drive. There were many things I didn't take for granted and this was one of them. I remember driving to work praising and thanking God for this privilege. For many years my husband drove me to work and home. At that time I enjoyed not having to deal with traffic, but when the time came for me to give up my comfort zone and drive, I experienced a freedom I didn't know existed. I enjoyed listening to my favorite Christian radio station. I was free to concentrate on prayer. I mean lots of prayer. I prayed, "Oh God, I pray for every person my eyes can see when I am driving and for every person I come in contact with throughout the day. You know what they are going through, so reveal yourself to them." I also said, "I will pray this prayer every day for the rest of my life." Do you understand what I just said? Every person my eyes fall upon will be prayed for until my graduation into heaven. What a prayer, I must say.

I now found myself dependent on others for transportation. My sisters, nieces and nephews made sure I kept all of my doctor appointments when Jon wasn't available.

The day finally came when hand controls were placed

in my car. I went to my first, and I can tell you my last, driving rehabilitation class. The therapist wanted me to have at least six hours of training. She didn't know about the driving lessons I had been giving myself in my neighborhood. She got in the car with me, Jon in the back, and told me where to drive, when to turn, when to stop, and other instructions. She immediately saw that I was well capable of operating my car and had adjusted very well with the hand controls. Her only problem with me was when she saw that I was driving with my foot on the gas and using the hand control for brakes only. I said, "This is how I want to drive." Just sitting behind the wheel and not using my feet didn't feel right. Besides, I still feel as if they are a part of my body. She finally gave her approval and told me I didn't have to return. Hallelujah! I passed! Now I can drive, drive, drive!

The Lord is good, a strong hold in the day of trouble; and he knoweth them that trust in him.
(Nahum 1:7, KJV)

The Lord is good. When trouble comes, he is the place to go to! And he knows everyone who trusts in him!
(Nahum 1:7, TLB)

Chapter Sixteen

When Reality Hits

Reality hits when I think about the people who are glad this happened to me. I always stood up for what I believed. I never compromised my walk in Christ. I have never been ashamed of the gospel of Jesus Christ. I have been laughed at, teased, called crazy and stupid. I know the kind of life I had without Christ. Even though life is much harder for me now, it's still better than going back into darkness.

Yes, I was constantly trying to improve myself. Yes, I spent many hours looking in the mirror. Yes, I finally liked the person I saw in that mirror. Yes, my body was dealt a heavy, vicious blow. Yes, I still have much hope and faith in Christ. And yes, I still believe in miracles.

Thank God I have people who really care for me and sadden over my afflictions.

CHRONIC PAIN IN HANDS AND LEGS

Reality hits me when I mistakenly hit the tips of my hands where the fingers use to be. What terrible pain I have to endure. It's like hitting your elbow with the pain magnified. I am sure most people have experienced this elbow pain. I live with this pain everyday. It's always there. With God's help, I can tune it out. My doctor says it will always be there, but I am standing on the scripture, "Therefore I tell you, whatever you ask for in prayer, believe that you have received it, and it will be yours." (Mark 11:24 Living Bible)   Listen to me! You can pray for anything and if you believe, you have it. It's yours! I believe that one day on this earth I will be free of this pain. I am so thankful for what's left of my hands right now.

I am also experiencing hit elbow-like pain in my legs too. Yes, it's always there, but worse. I call this pain shock pain. It occurs at any time. The pain starts from under my knee and travels down to what feels like my feet. This cannot be tuned out. I thank God that it only occurs once or twice a day. I have been taking pain medication for quite some time, but I have discontinued the use of it, because I didn't want to become addicted to it. This medication just made me drowsy anyway; it did nothing for my pain. I still believe one day this pain will no longer be a part of my body here on earth.

Reality hits when I have to deal with blisters. From time to time I get blisters on my legs when walking or standing too long. I then become my own nurse. While in the hospital, I observed the benefits of using saline to help heal wounds. Nurses would wet my legs down with saline three times a day, and with lots of prayers they were healed.   I took this knowledge and used it for myself. In about two weeks the blisters are gone until the next time. Thank God for prayer.

My mother would tell me, "Get off your feet and ride in your wheelchair!"   I couldn't, you see, I hated that chair! I'd rather get blisters than ride in it. I still hate it! I remember telling my physical therapist, "One day I will give this chair away." I thought for a few seconds and said, "Well, maybe it could be used at Disneyland." Wheelchair people don't have to deal with long lines in Disneyland; they get to go in through special lines. Thank God for wheelchairs at Disneyland.

TAKING SHOWERS

Reality hits when taking showers. I can no longer stand but I have to sit on a shower chair. The fear of falling comes to my mind every time I take off my legs. This scripture also comes to mind, "For the Holy Spirit, God's gift does not want you to be afraid of people, but to be wise and strong, and to love them and enjoy being with them." (II Timothy 1:7 Living Bible)

No longer can I enjoy closing my eyes in the tub and soaking my body in "Skin So Soft" bath oil. It made my body feel so special. It also makes your body soft and slippery. You know I can't use it on my shower chair, I might slip off. The thought of me falling flat on my face makes me angry and sad. My soaking in the tub days are over for now. I did say for now, you see, I believe my "Skin So Soft" days will return. Thank God for giving man the knowledge to make shower chairs.

MY HAIR

Reality hits very hard now that I am no longer able to perm my hair. I have always taken care of my hair starting in my teens. Now, I can't believe me, I have tried. It's hard holding combs, brushes and curlers when there are no fingers. I can no longer run my fingers through my hair, and no longer can I enjoy the pleasure of massaging my scalp. It's sad to say we take for granted little things that mean so much.

I now have to pay a stylist to perm my hair. But, I thank God for her. She is a Christian who loves Jesus. Frances is an answer to my prayers.

Thank God, I can comb and brush my hair. I can still touch up my hair with curlers too. I am blessed.

DRESSING

Reality hits me again when I am dressing. Taking off my legs to put on hose and shoes is a drag. The first time I went shopping for shoes was quite an experience.

As Jon and I approached the store thoughts were entering my mind, "Will I find the shoes I need? How am I going to put them on? I can't take my legs off, not in public!" I prefer shoes with rubber heels. The heels must be one and one-half inch in height. Flats are not recommended for prosthesis. I looked carefully through all of the shoes and found just the ones I needed. My wonderful husband got on his knees, took off my old shoes, and patiently wiggled the new shoes on to my feet. I kept the shoes on, put my old shoes in the box, paid the cashier, and was out the door.

I have no problem putting on dresses, but what about those dresses with zippers and buttons? Well, if the zipper is in the back I have to get help from Jon. When Jon isn't home I wear my clothes on backwards if it doesn't look too funny. Other times I zip my clothes up as far as I can, put on a topcoat until I get to my destination, and ask for assistance from a female. As for clothes with buttons, I was given a button closer and opener instrument in rehab. When I first saw the thing, I said to myself, "No way am I going to be able to use that." I saw how clumsy the therapist was when she demonstrated the use of it to me. I practiced and practiced over and over again, and became frustrated, until it finally clicked in my head. Now it is a snap. I can button my clothes only in the front.

Thank God I can use this instrument. Thank God for giving man the knowledge to make this instrument.

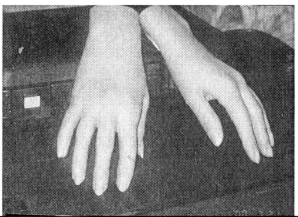

These hands were made for me.

EATING

Reality hits when it's time to dine out. Eating at home and around family is no problem to me, but it's a different story when dining out. My thoughts go back to the rehabilitation hospital when a doctor told me what to do when I dine out. She said, "When you dine out I suggest you wear gloves." I said to myself, "She must be kidding. How will I look wearing gloves at Wendy's or McDonalds?" I do have prosthesis hands, but they are very clumsy. I can't even move the fingers and they just get in the way, besides that, the zipper can be seen beneath the hands! I brought them home, tried them on one time and they have been in my Disney case since

1995.

Jon and I like Chinese food and we often eat out. The stares irritated me a little at first, but I would always talk to myself and say, "Remember when you couldn't feed yourself? How dare you feel this way!" The more I eat out, the better it gets. Besides, if it doesn't bother Jon, it shouldn't bother me.

VACATIONS

Reality hits when Jon takes me to our favorite vacation get-a-way, Disneyland. I now have to pack a wheelchair and a walking cane. Besides hating the wheelchair I also hate the walking cane. I now use the cane only when I have to walk up curbs, thank God. We have to request special rooms equipped for wheelchairs and with special equipment for bathroom showers.

Reality hits me when Jon pushes me through the crowds that I had previously enjoyed walking through so many times. We can no longer walk holding hands like other couples. I love Disneyland. I just thank God I have a husband who is not ashamed to travel with his wife in a wheelchair.

We have since traveled to the islands of Jamaica, Bahamas, the Florida Keys, San Francisco, and taken a cruise to Freeport Bahamas. We are also making plans for Hawaii.

PEOPLE STARES

Reality hits when I get stares at my hands; I must say that they do look weird. When shopping, the first thing I dread is paying the cashier and the stares of the people in line behind me. One look at my hands usually brings a surprised look, a pity look and sometimes a look of compassion. I get angry with myself for feeling embarrassed. I say to myself, "You should be thankful that you are even able to shop. Remember the hospital, the wheelchair?" I have to encourage myself a lot. I have learned to smile and say to cashiers, "Fingers are very important," and if there is time, an explanation is given as to what happened to me. Like I said earlier, I carry a picture of myself before my operations. I show it often and it makes me feel good. Thank God I still like to take pictures.

EXERCISING

Reality hits when it comes to exercising. Before my operations, I had always enjoyed exercising for good health. I rode my stationary bicycle, I used a rowing machine, and I jumped rope and enjoyed walking during my lunch period at work. Riding my bike isn't as much fun as it used to be because my feet fall off of the pedals. My rowing machine is very low to the floor and I can no longer stoop. Jump rope, of course, is out of the question. The days of walking on my lunch periods are over. It was so refreshing just being outside enjoying the sunshine and looking at the children on the playground, occasionally one child would yell, "Hi, Mrs. Burnam!" I would wave and continue walking.

My neighborhood is perfect for walking. All I can do now is watch the ladies take their daily walks laughing and talking as they pass my home. I'm thinking, "I would be right out there with them if things were different." Thank God I now have a new treadmill to exercise on. I am still walking.

SIGN LANGUAGE

Before losing my fingers one of my goals was to learn sign language. I wanted to be the first teacher to have a sign club. I knew the students would have fun learning to communicate with their hands instead of using their mouths. I also knew my church would eventually have need of a Signing Ministry, but thank God I am able to stand and greet at my church door.

THE PIANO

Many years ago, when we were little girls, my sister Joan and I took piano lessons for fifty cents. Yes, I did say fifty cents! We enjoyed our lessons, but eventually stopped when we got older. It has always been a dream of mine to resume taking lessons. I've always pictured myself entertaining the family at our gatherings and just playing for myself. It must be a wonderful feeling to sit down at a piano and get caught up in your own music. This is another dream I can't fulfill right now. Thank God I can shake the tambourine if I wanted to.

DRIVING

Reality hits again when I get behind the wheel. Just turning the key in the ignition hurts my hands. I have been told my hands will always be very sensitive. I know one day I will have fingers again. I believe in miracles. On every Friday after a long week of work I stopped at Wendy's on my way home to buy a large bag of fries and munch on them all the way home. How I miss that time. Driving is no longer fun. I now have to concentrate even more on what I am doing. I have to remember to use hand controls for the brakes and not my foot. I can still use my foot for the gas; it's another story trying to reach over for the brakes.

Reality also hits when I think of the many, many mornings of driving to work, seeing this homeless man walking down the sidewalk. He had been walking the same route for at least five or six years. He walked when it was cold, raining or sunny. My heart went out to him and my prayers. He was probably a husband and a father. "Oh, if only his relatives would come and take him home," were in my thoughts.

After his long journey back down the same street, he would stand on the corner about two blocks from where he was sleeping in the woods. I had to pass him every day on my way home. One day I noticed his shoes were very worn out. I decided right then and there that I would buy him some shoes; guessing his size was a big problem, and I prayed they would fit. That same day I saw him standing on the same corner, looking at all the cars passing him by. I often wondered what he was thinking. I pulled my car up close to where he was standing, rolled down the window, and handed the package to him. I don't remember hearing him say thank you. Along with the shoes, I placed a couple of dollars in the bag.

My heart continued to feel very sad for him. Seeing this man walking in the rain, cold and hot days made me feel worse. He was always in my prayers. One day while driving home the thought came to my mind, "I know what he needs. He needs a bicycle! Yes, a bicycle and I had just the bicycle in mind. You see every day I passed a little shop with used bicycles standing out front. I then said to myself, "You need to ride a bike for exercise. There they are." Little did I know the bike I would be buying wouldn't be for me but for a homeless man.

One day I finally stopped and purchased a bike. The owner placed it in the back of my Jeep and I was on my way, wondering, "How am I going to give this bike to him? I must get some help." I had been told this man was crazy and he was called Mr. Blanding because of the name of the street he walked on. I told my sister Marion what I wanted to do and asked for her assistance.

One evening we were driving down Blanding Boulevard hoping to see him on his corner, and there he was, not on the corner, but standing in front of a hamburger stand. We were told he stopped there every day waiting for a handout. We took the bicycle out of the truck and gave it to him. By this time we were the center of attention. The customers inside were looking, as well as the cars passing by. All of the people that traveled this road knew Mr. Blanding. He didn't say anything and we drove off. We glanced back and saw him walking with the bike. The next day I stopped by the hamburger stand, and asked one of the girls in the drive-through window, what happened after we left? She said that he left the bicycle there and the owner placed it in a shed for him. I never saw him with the bike. Maybe he had forgotten how to ride. Maybe he never knew. I lost track of Mr. Blanding when I went into the hospital. Now that I am out, he is nowhere in sight. I do hope my prayers were answered and he found his way back home.

EARLY MORNING PRAYER

Reality hits when my thoughts turn to the early Morning Prayer time with my prayer partner, Anne. We were always an hour early before school time. We prayed for our government, families, friends, the students, and our co-workers. Anne read devotions from the Guidepost Magazines, which left us with encouragement and peace in God's word. I felt peace in my room all throughout the day. How I miss that special time with Anne. I thank God for that special time in my life.

EMBARRASSMENT

Reality hits when I have traveled as far as Hawaii without any problems and returned home to face embarrassment.

On Saturdays, Jon and I have a regular routine which involves going to the grocery store, vegetable market, service station, and dry cleaners. I looked forward to these Saturdays because we were spending time together and the walking from the car to the buildings was good exercise, especially for me.

On this particular Saturday the weather was hot and that meant a lot of sweating, which is bad for me. You see, the rubber inserts in my prosthesis get moist and loose. I have to take them off and dry the inserts out.

We had been out for some time and Jon suggested we have lunch in this Chinese restaurant. My mind was far from sweating legs. We went in and chose the buffet. There were many choices of good foods to choose from.

We sat down and enjoyed our lunch. Our stomachs were full. All we needed now was to get home have a cup of decaf coffee, and rest.

After we finished our lunch Jon and I both got up from the table at the same time. I would always make sure the tables in the restaurants were strong enough for me to hold on to and pull myself up. If it is not steady, Jon helps me. The table passed my test, but as I pulled up my body seemed to twist to the right and before I knew it, I was on the floor! If that was not bad enough, my legs had come completely off! If only I was dreaming. Jon quickly pulled me up to my seat. Thank God he was strong enough. I remember saying, "How embarrassing!" The couple sitting behind us was shocked and puzzled. I heard the lady respond from my comment, "That's not the point!" Jon said, "Calm down and put your legs back on." He picked the legs up off the floor. Words cannot describe how I felt. I know the old Louise would have wanted to hide in a closet and cry so hard that my tears would have made Jon mad.

I got myself together and secured the first leg and then the other. All we could do was to look at each other with a smile and walk out laughing softly. We talked about how I had shocked the people in that restaurant and how I was the customer they would not wish to see again.

This incident brings me to my remembrance of a time when I was having throat problems. I was told that I had a hernia and this was the reason why I would be eating, and all of a sudden I would find myself choking. I was always aware of the problem and would eat small bites of food and drink plenty of water. When Jon and I would dine out, I would take my time and eat small bites. I always found myself getting up from the table and walking quickly to the restroom. I had to cough up the food lodged in my throat.

One evening I was sitting and I realized that I hadn't drunk any liquids. I wasn't having difficulties swallowing; and I heard a sweet voice that said, "You've been healed." I said, "Praise the Lord, I'm healed!"

The night before I had attended a service at New Covenant Ministries and had been prayed for. I have been able to eat in peace ever since that day. Praise God!

Continue earnestly in prayer, being vigilant in it with thanksgiving.

(Colossians 4:2, KJV)

Don't be weary in prayer; keep at it. Watch for God's answers and remember to be thankful when they come.

(Colossians 4:2, TLB)

Disneyworld trip in a wheelchair, in 1995

Chapter Seventeen

Expecting Miracles

I am expecting miracles from God. I also believe God can give me new fingers, legs and feet here on EARTH! Mark 11:24 says, *"Whatsoever things I desire, when I pray, believe I have received them and I shall have them."* I do believe there is nothing too big for God. Look at the sky! Isn't it amazing how the surgeon amputated my fingers one at a time and left two partial thumbs? I know who was controlling the knife.

I recovered because of my faith in a mighty God, praying family and friends, and a wonderful husband. I will never forget Jon's words when I told him he didn't marry me this way and that he was free to start a new life. He said, "Louise, nothing has changed." I know one day he will make Jesus Lord of his life.

On January 26, 1992, I wrote in the front of my Bible these words, "Jesus is Lord of my life no matter what happens to me, I can take it, because Jesus lives big in me."

Get strong and rooted in God's Word; you never know which road you are going to have to travel through, and only God can take you through it.

I am more than a conqueror through him that loves me; and since God is for me, who can be against me?

(Romans 8:37, KJV)

But despite all this, overwhelming victory is ours through Christ who loved us enough to die for us.

(Romans 8:37, TLB)

Chapter Eighteen

Why Me, Lord?
Why Me?

Many are the afflictions of the righteous but the Lord God delivers him out of them all.

(Psalm 34:19, KJV)

The good man does not escape all troubles-he has them too. But the Lord helps him in each and every one.

(Psalm 34:19, TLB)

The righteous cry, and the Lord heareth, and delivereth them out of all their troubles.

(Psalm 34:17, KJV)

Yes, the Lord hears the good man when he calls to him for help, and saves him out of all his troubles.

(Psalm 34:17, TLB)

I waited patiently for the Lord; and he inclined unto me, and heard my cry.

(Psalm 40:1, KJV)

I waited patiently for God to help me; then he listened and heard my cry.

(Psalm 40:1, TLB)

Be pleased, O Lord, to deliver me: O Lord, make haste to help me. Let them be ashamed and confounded together that seek after my soul to destroy it; let them be driven backward and put to shame that wish me evil. Let them be desolate for a reward of their shame that say unto me, Aha, aha.

(Psalm 40:13-15, KJV)

Please, Lord, rescue me! Quick! Come and help me! Confuse them! Turn them around and send them sprawling – all these who are trying to destroy me. Disgrace the scoffers with their utter failure.

(Psalm 40:13-15, TLB)

Be merciful unto me, O God: for man would swallow me up; he fighting daily oppresseth me. Mine enemies would daily swallow me up: for they be many that fight against me, O thou most High. What time I am afraid, I will trust in thee. In God I will praise his word, in God I have put my trust; I will not fear what flesh can do unto me.

(Psalm 56:1-4, KJV)

Lord, have mercy on me; all day long the enemy troops press in, so many are proud to fight against me; how they long to conquer me But when I am afraid, I will put my confidence in your. Yes, I will trust the promises of God. And since I am trusting him, what can mere man do to me?

(Psalm 56:1-4, TLB)

I know now that some of us have to go through more afflictions than others. One day I will find out why when I graduate into Heaven.

Fight the good fight of faith, lay hold on eternal life, whereunto thou art also called, and hast professed a good profession before many witnesses.

(1 Timothy 6:12, KJV)

Fight on for God. Hold tightly to the eternal life which God has given you, and which you have confessed with such a ringing confession before many witnesses.

(1 Timothy 6:12, TLB)

Chapter Nineteen

I Can Still Write

When I was in rehab my physical therapist encouraged me to start practicing my handwriting. I am so glad she did, because if I hadn't, I probably wouldn't be able to write this book today. Thank God for her encouragement.

It wasn't hard for me to think of what to write about. It had to be about Jesus. I was given a pen and a tablet and I put my thoughts on paper. Thank you, Jesus. I had enough strength in my hand to write. Thank you, Jesus for giving me the strength to write this book.

Death and life are in the power of the tongue: and
they that love it shall eat the fruit thereof.
(Proverbs 18:21, KJV)

Those who love to talk will suffer the consequences.
Men have died for saying the wrong thing.
(Proverbs 18:21, TLB)

Practice Writing after Operation
I love Jesus

I love to go to Church

Jesus Is Lord of my
life

Jesus Is Lord

Jesus Loves me

My current manuscript
I love Jesus.

I love to go to church.

Jesus is Lord of my life.

Jesus is Lord.

Jesus loves me.

My current cursive writing

I love Jesus.
I love to go to church.
Jesus is Lord of my life.
Jesus is Lord.
Jesus loves me.

Thank you Jesus!

Louise Holzendorf Burnam

Chapter Twenty

Scripture Dreams

SEPTEMBER 1999

Now unto him that is able to do exceeding abundantly above all that we ask or think, according to the power that worketh in us.

(Ephesians 3:20, KJV)

Now glory be to God who by his mighty power at work within us is able to do far more than we would ever dare to ask or even dream of-infinitely beyond our highest prayers, desires, thoughts, or hopes.

(Ephesians 3:20, TLB)

THURSDAY, OCTOBER 10, 1999, AT 8:30 AM

Abide in me, and I in you.

(John 15:4, KJV)

Take care to live in me, and let me live in you.

(John 15:4, TLB)

Also on October 14, 1999 in this dream I received my healing. I had my new fingers and my new legs. What a wonderful feeling! What a wonderful dream!

Chapter Twenty-One

Update

Praise God! I am walking without my cane! I can walk up curbs without assistance. I have new prosthesis, which doesn't call for the uncomfortable waist straps. Hallelujah! My waist is free from welts! The blisters are gone because of rubber attachments, and there is no rubbing. These legs really feel like part of my body. My new doctor is amazed over how well I can walk with the prosthesis. The only downside of them is the sweating because of the rubber. Thank God for the rubber. My hands remind me every day to give thanks to God. They remind me to tell people about the love of Jesus whenever I can. I still can't wear the hands that were made for me. Oh yes, we made that trip to Hawaii. What a wonderful trip. I pushed my wheelchair with our luggage in the seat all through the airports. I didn't have to ride in it, not one time! Our trip consisted of ten airplane rides. You know what that means, remember my traveling prayer? I saw and came in contact with many lives that will be changed in my future.

On April 24th, 2001, God blessed me with a new home in a Country Club on the golf course, H A L L E L U J A H! I am still waiting patiently for my body's miracle. Remember the scripture in:

Now unto him that is able to do exceeding abundantly above all that we ask or think according to the power that worketh in us.
(Ephesians 3:20, KJV)

Now glory be to God who, by his mighty power at work within us, is able to do far more than we could ever dare to ask or even dream of infinitely beyond our highest prayers, desires, thoughts or hopes.
(Ephesians 3:20, TLB)

Take therefore no thought for the morrow, for the morrow shall take thought for the things of itself.
(Matthew 6:34, KJV)

So don't be anxious about tomorrow. God will take care of your tomorrow too. Live one day at a time.
(Matthew 6:34, TLB)

Chapter Twenty-Two

Something to Think About

THE CROSS

My husband and I finally made that trip to Hawaii. During one of our sightseeing adventures on the Island of Kauai, Jon drove up to a small jewelry store. As he pulled up to park the car he told me that he would be right back. While he was walking into the jewelry store, I said to God, "I want that cross in the window. Let him come out of the door with a cross for me." I saw four or five different ones but the white one caught my eye. As you know by now white is my favorite color. When Jon came back to the car he handed me a small bag. I opened it, and to my surprise inside was a small box with a cross inside. I was so surprised. This couldn't be happening! A cross from Jon? It wasn't the white one but just getting a cross from my husband was a miracle! You see, I'm talking about a man who dislikes Christian music and TV. Yet, here he is giving me a cross! I feel God is telling me, "I hear your prayers. Keep on praying, Louise."

Jon has truly demonstrated the meaning of love to me. He is and has been a very good husband.

The harvest truly is plenteous, but the Labourers are few; pray that he will send forth Labourers into his harvest.

(Matthew 9:37-38, KJV)

"The harvest is so great, ant the workers are so few," he told his disciples, "So pray to the one in charge of the harvesting, and ask him to recruit more workers for his harvest fields."

(Matthew 9:37-38, TLB)

And they said, Believe on the Lord Jesus Christ, and thou shalt be saved, and thy house.

(Acts 16:31, KJV)

They replied, "Believe on the Lord Jesus and you will be saved and your entire household."

(Acts 16:31, TLB)

THINKING OF OTHERS

When people with amputations come across your path in life, make conversation with them. Do not just stare and feel sorry for the individuals. Get them to talk about their condition. Ask how it feels to have a limb or limbs missing from their body. Ask how they deal with it mentally. Most of all find out if they are saved and if not please tell them about the love of Jesus. They must be told that only Jesus can put joy and peace into their lives.

Losing limbs that were once part of your body can be devastating to an individual, especially to a nonbeliever.

Sometimes my body feels disconnected. It is the only way I can describe this feeling:
DIS.....CON.....NEC.....TED

When I experience this feeling, I pray and encourage myself in the Lord until it is gone. What does the non-believer do? Cry? Curse? Get high? Blame God? Get depressed?

I thank God for His peace. How can you experience this peace? Just pray, "Jesus, I believe you are the Son of God. I repent of my sins. Thank You for forgiving me of my sins. Thank You for coming into my heart. Thank You for saving me."

We are troubled on every side yet not distressed;
We are perplexed, but not in despair; persecuted,
but not forsaken; cast down, but not destroyed.
(2 Corinthians 4:8, KJV)

We are pressed on every side by troubles, but not
crushed and broken. We are perplexed because
we don't give up and quit. We are hunted down
but God never abandons us. We get knocked
down, but we get up again and keep going.
(2 Corinthians 4:8, TLB)

Chapter Twenty-Three

Imagining the Operation

Sometimes I find myself imagining what the scene may have been like in the operating room when my fingers and legs were taken from me. I don't know why these thoughts come to me, but after forming a picture in my mind, I don't feel sad. It's as if I am finally involved in this decision.

I see an operating room with big, bright lights shining over a long narrow cot. I see a man at the head of the cot with a mask on controlling a machine. He is the anesthesiologist. I see two female nurses or doctors on my left side looking down at me and two doctors on my right side. I see a patient on this narrow cot. Oh my God, it's me! I'm on the cot! I'm going to have an operation! I'm going to have my fingers taken from me! I see a saw-like instrument. The surgeon picks it up. One of the nurses pulls back the sheet from my legs. The doctor looks at the anesthesiologist. He nods his head, which means, you may proceed, she is out. The surgeon begins with the right leg. He saws and saws through my flesh. The blood is running everywhere and the nurses try to contain it! The leg is finally amputated and the other doctor picks it up and places it on a table. He begins to staple up what's left of my right leg. Then the leg is bandaged up.

Next, the surgeon walks around to my left side. It's time to amputate the left leg. He picks up the instrument and begins sawing through my flesh again. When he completes the amputation, the left leg is given to his assistant and it is placed on the table next to the right leg. What a bloody mess! I see blood everywhere! The nurses try to clean me up as fast as they can. After I am cleaned up one nurse picks up the staple machine and begins stapling and bandaging what's left of my leg.

By this time sadness comes over everyone in the room. Their faces seem to say: "This is terrible! Couldn't someone have done something to prevent this horrible scene?" After speaking a few words to his assistant the doctor picks up a smaller saw and goes after my fingers on my right hand. The sawing is very swift. He starts with: my first finger, Zip! The second finger, Zip! The third finger, Zip! The fourth finger, Zip! When he gets to the fifth finger, the thumb, he says to himself, "Maybe I can cut off part of her thumb and hope the infection will stop at the cut." He leaves part of the thumb and I'm saying "Praise God." The fingers are stapled up.

The surgeon now walks around to my left hand. He starts with: the first finger, Zip! The second finger, Zip! The third finger, Zip! The fourth finger, Zip! When he got to the thumb he says to himself, "I've got to try to save part of this thumb too. She needs a grip on this hand also." I'm saying, "Praise the Lord! Praise the Lord!" He cuts off part of the thumb, hoping the infection will stop at the cut. I am a bloody mess. My fingers are stapled up. The doctor looks at his assistant, shakes his head and walks out of the room. Tears come into the eyes of the nurses. I am rolled into ICU (Intensive Care Unit). The scene is over once again in my mind, until the next time.

Thank God for the surgeon who obeyed the voice in his heart which said not to cut all of her thumbs off because she will need a grip. Thank You, God!

Take therefore no thought for the morrow, for the morrow shall take thought for the things of itself.
(Matthew 6:34, KJV)

So don't be anxious about tomorrow. God will take care of your tomorrow too. Live one day at a time.
(Matthew 6:34, TLB)

Chapter Twenty-Four

The Nightmare Through Family and Friends

MY MOTHER

When I was told the doctors wanted to amputate Louise's fingers and legs because of infections, I knew her husband had no choice but to give his consent. My husband developed gangrene in his legs when he was alive, and I always felt it could have been avoided if the doctors had reacted sooner. But now my daughter was facing the same operations, only she went farther, her fingers too. I knew Louise had much faith and love for Jesus and I knew He would always be with her. My prayers were answered. It's amazing to see what God has done for her. It's also amazing to see her writing, walking, cooking and doing so many things. I have had many prayers answered.

This scripture comes to my mind, Matthew 7:7, *"Ask, and you will be given what you ask for. Seek, and you will find. Knock, and the door will be opened."* Louise is a miracle. Thank You, God.

MY BROTHER CLARENCE HOLZENDORF

When my sister Betty called and told my wife and me the horrible news that Louise was in a coma, I couldn't believe it. I was heart broken and felt terrible. I said to myself, "Not my sister Louise! She is so kind, thoughtful and generous. With her loving and sincere faith in the Lord Jesus Christ, How could this be happening to her?" I immediately prayed to God for her healing. I truly believed she recovered because of her genuine faith in God.

MY SISTER-IN-LAW, BERTHA HOLZENDORF

Louise, I love you and your husband as my sister and brother in Christ.

My first thoughts when I heard of your illness were disbelief. You are a loving person, always thoughtful of others and the most beautiful person to know. How could this be happening? I knew you were a child of God. I knew that this was not of God. So this is when my profession was in question.

1. How and why did the doctors who cared for you let this happen?

2. How could a staff in a well-known hospital that were supposed to have been trained not do their job? I was really puzzled and disappointed.

3. I told my husband to make sure the doctors and staff were doing everything for you and to question all and everything about your treatment. My profession failed you in your medical care, but God has not.

Thank God for your husband, family and friends, and most of all thank God for your brother Clarence Holzendorf, Sr. Know that each and every day he prayed for you. He felt and suffered what was happening to you. I know he loves you and sees you as a child of God.

Louise, our system failed you. I'm so sorry and ask God to forgive all those involved.

In God we love and trust. Your sister-in-law, Bertha Holzendorf.

BETTY HOLZENDORF EDDY

When you called me and asked me to write down what I had experienced when you were going through that difficult time in your life that started on December 9, 1994, I thought I could never put those feelings into words. But as I sat down to write, the Lord started revealing things to me. I experienced a new revelation of what God's Word says to me and that I could cast all my cares on Him. The night you called me from the hospital, I could tell by the sound of your voice that this was serious. Besides, this was going to be a special season and you were supposed to be here. It was soon to be Mother's and your birthday. The Christmas Holidays were coming up and I could always look forward to you sending out special words of encouragement and leading the family in a fast for the season and the coming New Year. So you and I agreed during that phone conversation that you would be healed, we bound up the enemy and agreed that God did not give us a spirit of fear, but of power, love and a sound mind. A mind that would always stay focused on Him. From that time on, everything seemed like a dream. I went through the holidays, but I don't remember much about them...that time came and went so fast. I remember coming to the hospital every day, praying and some days fasting for you. Most of the time there was someone else with me in your room. We would ask the doctor or nurse or whoever was in your room, how you were doing. We asked how much breathing the respirator did for you. We would listen for you to breathe with every bit of hope that we had and if the hospital staff didn't have any, we would encourage them because we knew that there were ministering angels all around you and God had you in the palm of His hand. There were people all over Jacksonville praying for you. Thank God for praying, faith-believing people. Those people that can go to the throne room of God, intercede in the Spirit, and ask for healing.

So, one day, praise be to God, you started to breathe on your own. That was good news, but the bad news was that there was no circulation in your hands or feet. I thought, this is just too much Lord, why does she have to go through this? Surely, the doctors knew a way to start the circulation again, besides we are and were a praying family and God had heard our prayers and you were going to be healed. Not realizing that the healing God had for you had not yet manifested itself and that in the end God would get the glory. So when Jon, your husband, called us over to Joan's house one night to tell us what the doctor needed to do in order to save your life, I did not want to believe what I was hearing. We all cried. I did not want the thought of seeing you without hands and feet to enter into my mind.

I thought back to the time when our sister Kenneth was in a car accident and suffered a broken neck and how God healed her of that. When I was going through depression, God healed me of that. When we went through the death of our father, God healed our hearts. When we asked the Lord to deliver our brother of alcohol, He did it. Through all of this, God gave our mother the power and strength to endure. I thought to myself, Lord you have got to deliver us again. Well, the day of your surgery did come and it was one of the saddest days of my life, but when it was all over, I saw such a determination in you to live, I know you wanted to show that the devil was a liar. I know you wanted to let the world know that whatever you have left after your surgery, you would use it to praise and glorify God. I knew that you would walk again, to the glory of God, and tell the good news. I was at a funeral not so long ago; it was the first baby funeral I had attended. Written on the back of the program was a poem about God calling the baby back home to be an angel to watch over someone else. My heart went out to that mother because if I had believed that God had taken my baby, I would have cried out, "Why me, Lord? Not my child." When you asked God why you, did you hear Him say why not you. Did He say no matter what the enemy has done to you, I will still get the glory and no weapon formed against me shall prosper?

Louise, when these minor afflictions hit me I think about your love for God and the strength that he gave you and how you are not ashamed of the Gospel. It made me know that I can do all things through Christ who strengthened me. Since Joan is no longer with us, I want you to know that she was a pillar of stone for you. She stayed in your room many nights. She was always there for you, she would call us to her house and we would pray and intercede for you. She would encourage us to fast and would let no negative conversation go on in the room. I do have to admit that there was a time in your room when I almost lost it and Joan said to me, "Don't let Louise see you that way." So I got myself together and listened to what the doctors were saying. Joan, I miss you.

After your surgery, I would come to your room and

sometimes I would feel very sorry for you. You would always have an encouraging word for me. You said to me one time, "Look at me, I am going to make it and so can you." Louise, if I ever did anything to offend you in any way, even if I was not there enough for you, especially during your recovery, please forgive me. I want you to know that as a child of God, you are always on God's mind and you are my hero. Unlike Princess Diana, who was a great humanitarian, but much like Mother Theresa, who was not only a great humanitarian, but knew God too. You will touch the lives of many people with the good news. They will know that when you accepted God into your life, you were truly born again into a royal family. That is, the family of God. Our God will do what He said He would do.

And Lord, as I write this, my prayer is that if anybody was offended by what was said or done during those times when faith and patience were weak, I pray that they receive a healing of any hurt that was done unto them. I pray they forgive the person or persons so that they can be restored into the family of God and be renewed and filled with your unconditional love, in Jesus' name. Amen.

We must always keep our mind on God in the midst of all of our troubles. God is El Shaddai (Multi-God) and Jehovah jireh, our provider in time of healing and needs and Jehovah shalom, He gives us peace and patience to stand and He will never leave us because He is Jehovah shammah and will always be here.

I love you and thank God for you. Thanks to your husband Jon for being there for you, and thanks to my husband Clifford and my children for being there for me.

LOUISE'S VICTORY BY KENNETH MAE HOLZENDORF HENDERSON

Louise is my dearest sister. We are three years apart in age but she has been always been very special to me. I remember being at home talking to her and sharing secrets. When my husband and I eloped, Jon and Louise kept our secrets. When our children were born (all four) Abram and I had a difficult time with our finances. I worked and guess who provided me with clothes? Louise made sure I had something to wear every day. Thank God for Louise. When I needed money who did I turn to? Louise. So you can see that Louise affected every part of my life with her loving and caring spirit.

Louise became ill in December of 1994 at the end of the year. She had a cold and felt very bad one night. She told Jon she needed to go to the hospital. She was admitted and I remembered going to see her when she began to get worse. They said that she had pneumonia. She was also placed in a coma so that she would lay still. We learned that her lungs were like cardboard and that the machine was keeping her alive. Boy, what a shocker. It happened so suddenly.

My sister Joan called the family to pray. We all gathered in the name of Jesus to intercede for my sister so that she would be healed in Jesus' name. During our prayer, our sister Marion experienced a cough and hurting in her chest. We proclaimed it as Louise's healing (that was a move of the Holy Spirit). Marion did not know what had happened to her. We told her afterward. She took on your feeling (true intercession).

The next day we were told that her lungs were looking better. A miracle from God! Louise's body blew up double her size, and she did not look like Louise. Her hands and feet were always so cold. We noticed as they began to turn black, but no one did anything!

Joan came to my house to tell me the terrible news. Louise would have to have her hands and legs removed because they had died on her. My God I was overwhelmed with grief. I howled and screamed, "Oh no, they cannot do that to her! She would not want this done!" This was the first time in my life I had displayed such emotions in front of others. My husband Abram was there also trying to comfort me.

The next day they proceeded with the amputations. Before the surgery, Joan got our sister-in-law Betty to ask Louise if this is what she wanted. She replied, "I want to live!" Praise God for my sister's strength in the midst of a troubling situation!

Jon was always faithful making all of the right decisions when we could not because we were tied up in emotions. Jon kept his head!

You must understand, God had healed Louise's lungs so she was able to go through the operation. They did not have to amputate her hands, but her fingers, praise God! Her recovery was remarkable! Can you believe she never, ever complained or said why me? Tell me if that's not the strength of God. Jesus, her personal Savior, kept her from freaking out. Thank You, Lord!

All of the nurses and doctors were amazed over her recovery. They had expected her to die. That was why no one cared about her hands and feet deteriorating on her. They all now say she is a miracle. No one believed she would leave the hospital, get over the pain of amputations, walk, or use her hands.

Louise had so many people praying for her. Now she

walks, goes shopping, and drives her car. A MIRACLE, THAT'S WHAT MY SISTER IS! SHE LOVES JESUS!

MY VERSION OF HOW JOAN FELT ABOUT LOUISE'S ORDEAL

My sister Joan went home to be with the Lord on January 11, 1997. She did not write down her experiences about Louise, so I ask the Holy Spirit to reveal to me Joan's heart. At the time of Louise's illness Joan was separated from her husband. She devoted all her time making sure Louise was being properly taken care of by the doctors and nurses. So every day after school she would go to the hospital. She began to ask if there was anyone else who can help? I told her has God blessed her to have the time and that this was her season to be there for Louise. Emotionally Joan went through it believing God for Louise's recovery. You could see the pain on her face (Joan's) hurting for Louise and having faith that Louise was going to pull through.

We would gather at Joan's house to pray for Louise's recovery. The doctors had given up on her. We asked God for His perfect will and God heard our cry, especially Joan's. She would anoint her with oil and lay her hands on her. She was always interceding on Louise's behalf. Thank God for Joan's love and faithfulness for her sister.

LOUISE'S COUSIN SARAH HOLZENDORF PRINDLE

At first I did not know Louise was in the hospital. I later heard she was in the hospital by our cousin Jessie.

I began to ask God to let His will be done and raise her up. One day I was at the bus terminal and saw her brother King Jr. I asked him how Louise was getting along. He said that she is just there, but I knew it was someone else there too. JESUS! Jesus said He will never leave us nor forsake us. You see, he was with her all the time because he raised her up.

Her mother gave Louise my phone number. She called me, came to see me and brought me medicine for my arthritis. Louise also sends me cards on occasions. Oh, Louise is a child of God! Everything she asks God for He gives it to her.

Louise is an inspiration to me. Louise is a miracle! A walking miracle! O thank God! He can do anything! Nothing is too hard for God. "Hast thou not known? Hast thou not heard that the everlasting God, the creator of the end of the earth, fainteth not? There is no searching of his understandings. Even the youth shall faint and be weary, and the young men shall utterly fall. But they that wait upon the Lord shall renew their strength. They shall mount up with wings as eagles, they shall run and not be weary, they shall walk and not faint." Isaiah 40:38-31

Oh yes, Louise brought me a lovely houseplant and also an exercise bike. Now this is love. She is always showing love, for God is LOVE.

Louise, you have kept the faith and are now running the race with patience.

May God bless you always and smile on you.

Your Cousin, Sarah Holzendorf Prindle

MY SIDE OF THE STORY
BY DEBBIE COOPER

I'll never forget that day December 9, 1994. Joan, Louise's sister, came into my classroom and told me that Louise was admitted into the hospital with pneumonia. I did not think it was serious at the time, because people are in and out of the hospital all the time with pneumonia. Then I began thinking that it must be bad, because Louise is a person who never told anyone when she was sick.

After work, Joan and I went straight to the hospital. Louise was sitting up in the bed talking to Jon her husband. I felt relieved because it looked as if she was doing fine, although she was having some problems breathing and was using an oxygen mask off and on. We left the hospital feeling that she was going to be fine.

The next day Joan came to my classroom looking worried. She told me that Monique, her daughter, called her and said that Louise was put in the Intensive Care Unit. I could not believe this! I did not understand what had happened! She was doing fine, I thought.

We got substitutes to cover our classes, picked up my husband Charles from work and went straight to the hospital. When we arrived at Louise's room, she was on full oxygen and could not talk to us. I couldn't believe this was happening. Instead of her getting better, she was getting worse. Because her breathing became more difficult three days later, Louise was placed in a coma on life support.

I went to the hospital every day. We were on Christmas break, so we did not have to worry about going back to work. The Lord always made a way. This made it possible for one of us to be with Louise at all times. Louise's husband Jon stayed with her every night and all through the day. He was there whenever he had a break from work. We prayed and read the Word of God to her all day. As I prayed to God to bring Louise back to us, I could not imagine Louise not being with us anymore. I also questioned God, wondering, why is this happening to her? Louise loves the Lord. She always put Him first in her life; she talked about Him and lifted Him up all the time. I did not know why she was going through this.

One morning while Louise's sister, Marion and I were praying. I saw Louise's hand on the side of the bed and lifted the covers. I looked at her hands; they were all black and blue on each finger. I told Marion to look and then I pulled the cover off of her feet they were also black and blue on every toe. I knew this was bad and asked what is being done about it? No one gave me any answers. I believed the doctors did not think Louise was going to live so they did not do anything to help the circulation in her hands and feet.

I started crying that day because I did not think she was coming back to us. Yes, I have faith! I love the Lord Jesus and I am a born again Christian. But I also have feelings. Louise's brother-in-law Abram, who is married to her sister Kenneth, came to town that day. I was crying when he came into the hospital room. He told me that I needed to get control of myself. I thought to myself, what does he mean? There was nothing else I could do.

Every day and night the family got together at the hospital or over Joan's house and prayed. We would not give the devil the victory of taking her from us. We knew that it would take the healing power of Jesus to bring her back.

One day while praying at Joan's house I wondered, should we be holding on to Louise? Is she supposed to go? Should we let her go? The doctors did not give us any hope and they did not believe she would make it much longer. Even one of the nurses told me that people in this condition never make it.

On December 19, we had some good news. Louise's temperature decreased; the infection was clearing and the respirator was down to sixty, even though she was still getting one hundred percent oxygen.

We did not do much to celebrate Christmas that year. We traditionally gathered at different family members' houses. This year all we did was to make sure the children had gifts and acknowledge Jesus' birthday.

In late December Jon called a family meeting. All adults were present except for Mother, Louise's mother. She could not take the pressure of what was going on. Jon told us that the doctors said that the only way Louise would have a chance to live was to bring her out of the coma and amputate her fingers and legs. Everyone was in shock and did not want this to happen. While everyone was expressing their feelings, my mind began to wander. Louise is so pretty. She is always doing things to make herself even prettier. She would not want to look like that. What would she do? She always told us to always put on make-up and fix our hair. I knew in my mind that this had to be done, but I could not picture her like this.

After everyone calmed down Jon said, "I am not asking for your permission, but I am telling you that I have already made the decision to have the amputation to save her life." He also said that he wanted his wife to live and did not care what she looked like. He gave us the respect by telling us first, even though he had already made the decision. No one knew that Jon had already talked to Mother. He was keeping her up to date every day. She already knew what was going on and had agreed with Jon that this had to be done.

The next day Louise's brother, King Holzendorf and his wife Betty came to the hospital. When they asked Louise if she wanted to have the amputations she shook her head and said yes. She wanted to live.

The amputations had occurred and Louise was improving every day. I remember going into her hospital room one morning after the amputations. She was sitting up in her bed. I asked her what I can do to help her. She wanted me to brush her teeth. I realized that she could not do anything for herself without fingers or legs. I had never helped a person who was sick before. I was nervous and afraid, but I did it and it made me feel good inside to be able to help. Her sister Joan, who is now in heaven, was a God-send. She visited with Louise more than any of us. She had more time to be with her and was able to do more with her. I did what I could to help, even though I knew it was not enough. Louise was always so independent. She is a miracle from God and she seems to amaze me every day.

Debbie Cooper, Niece

MARION HOLZENDORF HUNTER

For the Lord is a sun and shield, the Lord will give grace and glory: *No good thing will he withhold from them that walk uprightly*, Psalm 84:11

To sit and put into words about how God healed and set my sister free is exciting. It is encouraging to testify of God's goodness and grace toward us, not to mention His never ending love for his children. We must remember that Satan is always on the opposite side trying to discourage God's children. Satan is a liar and the father of lies from the foundation of the world.

The month of December is an exciting and busy month. Louise is officially known as the family M.C., secretary, and referee (all in one). She schedules family nights on a calendar, reminds us about birthdays to celebrate, and most of all reminds all that Jesus is the reason for it all.

I received a call from my sister, Joan, (who has gone home to be with our Lord Jesus Christ) at my job, telling me that Louise had been checked into the hospital that night before due to breathing problems. She stated that she was fine and would see me there later. We agreed in the name of Jesus for her healing. I stayed in prayer – praying in the Holy Ghost all that day. For the word says in 1 Thessalonians 5:17, *"Pray without ceasing."* We gathered there in her room that night, the whole gang (family). Louise sat up in bed, feeling great and talking to everyone-making statements such as, "I'll be at work on Monday." John 10:10 says, *"The thief cometh not but for to steal, and to kill, and to destroy."* He had another plan. See, Satan doesn't play by rules. He doesn't even know how. I once heard a mighty man of God say from the Holy Ghost that if you make a deposit you can make a withdrawal at anytime, when needed. Louise is and was at that time a Christian.

Little did I know that I would have my own revelation on this statement. A few days later Louise was in a state of unconsciousness, with very little breathing on her own, therefore she was breathing with the help of a machine (the prefix UN meaning to do the contrary or reverse, to deprive of or remove from). These words describe what Satan had in mind for Louise to deprive her of the "B" clause of John 10:10, *"I am come that they* (she) *might have life and that they* (she, Louise) *might have it more* (in fullest measure) *abundantly."*

As I rushed to her bedside morning and evening, I spoke the Word over her. I spoke life to her spirit.

1 Peter 5:8 said to me,

Be sober, be vigilant, because your adversary the devil, as a roaring lion, walketh about, seeking whom he MAY devour.

I told Satan that you would not have this child of God. You will not have my sister, in the name of Jesus. Look at the key words that were given to my spirit AS and MAY. The Word told me he was not really a vigorous lion, but he would love to be one and he's asking permission may I devour you. I thanked God for good sound Holy Ghost teaching that came back to my remembrance. Morning and evening I sat beside Louise for days, praying in the Holy Ghost and reading scriptures to her spirit. You see, Louise's emotions were not alive, but her spirit was alive. We communicated through the spirit. I knew she heard every word I said. There were many times when all of us (family) would have a Holy Ghost good time singing, preaching and laughing about how God would raise her off that bed. We gathered at Joan's and my home to intercede for Louise. When you praise and worship God for who He is when you're in your season of prosperity, healing, and happiness, if by any means Satan tries to attack you, you will come out in victory. This is and was the revelation that God gave me about Louise; she made many deposits and even though she could not pray for herself the intercessors' job was easy. I knew she was at peace somewhere. The word that Louise had given to herself day in and day out was and is quick and powerful and sharper than any two-edged sword piercing even to the dividing asunder of soul and spirit and of the joints and marrow and is a discerner of the thoughts and intents of the heart, Hebrews 4:12. Louise knew her Healer and Creator. Her Creator knew her soul and spirit. He knows her thoughts and He knew what her intents would be after He helped her off that bed of afflictions with healing all through her joints and marrow, the healing that Satan tried to stop by stopping the flow of blood going through. You see that blood was Jesus' blood in Louise's body and Satan hates Jesus. My eyes would travel up and down her lifeless blue and purple hands and legs praying, never once in doubt of my God's power.

Many days later my sisters and I were in intensive prayer. Doctors began to talk doubt saying that she will never awaken or breathe on her own; so try to accept this act of God. I spoke and thanked them replying, "She is in God's hand and we appreciate everything you've done so far. She will breathe on her own because the act of God is in ACTION NOW HEALING HER BODY." Some friends began to speak doubt and unbelief. I removed myself from them. For faith comes by hearing, and hearing the Word of God, not hearing opinions. Many days followed and my sister and I never gave up.

One Friday night while we were in Joan's home interceding, God visited us there. His sweet, sweet spirit entered and smiled. Can you imagine a critical moment and God is smiling? Now at that moment I was not aware of the fact that he was not aware of the fact that He was smiling, but, hours later He showed me his glory.

Rivers of living water flowed from my mouth as the Spirit himself made intercession for us with moanings and groanings which cannot be uttered. I laid down the flesh in order for the Holy Ghost to get the perfect will of God. The mask of fluid that lined Louise's lungs began to flow from my lungs at one period of travailing, and I could not breathe clearly. I grasped for breath. My family was aware and Joan reached out and covered me with prayer. I was not aware of others around me. The spirit only ministered to let me know that Louise's lungs had an opening in them and we began to praise and thank God for Jesus' healing power through shouting, crying, singing, and worshipping him.

The Spirit instructed us not to go out to the hospital that night, but have faith and believe that God is faithful.

The next morning I wanted to jump up and be there bright and early. I moved in faith slowly. My sister Joan couldn't wait. The phone rang and she shouted, "Marian, she's breathing 40 percent on her own!" I jumped for joy, finished dressing, and drove to the hospital. Everybody was there and we praised God in her room and His glory was known in that Intensive Care Unit by the doctors and nurses.

My last and final mission with Louise was to speak to her spirit about loving herself, loving the whole beautiful woman God had made to love life, to love wanting to be around people, and most of all to show the love for her God.

Many days later I sat and spoke these confessions to her spirit until the day she breathed 100% on her own. Praise God!

Beloved think it not strange concerning the fiery trail which is to try you, as though some strange thing will happen unto you. But rejoice, inasmuch as you are partakers of the Christ's sufferings; that, when his glory shall be revealed, you may be glad also with exceeding joy.

(1 Peter 4:12)

KENNETH JOHNSON, LOUISE'S AUNT

As I sit and try to put into words how I felt during Lousie's hardest moments in her life, I find that it's not easy to do; but this is what I did: I prayed daily for God to heal her body, and I called my sister, which is her mom, Bernice, daily waiting to hear a good report. I never gave up on her because our God does not give up on us.

Prayer changes situations in life. To see Louise today driving, walking, and shopping is a great joy to me.

Love, Kenneth Johnson, Aunt

MUZETTA BUTLER, LOUISE'S AUNT

Contemplating on what type of recovery my youthful niece would have, I began to focus on the miracle he was about to do. I can recall praying around the clock seeking prayer with and from surrounding family and friends. I knew when two or more of us touched and agreed in Jesus' name, something had to happen.

Today, I see a miracle. I see what can happen through the "Power of Prayer." I am reminded of something I once heard. P U S H, meaning, Pray-Until-Something-Happens. The gift of life was renewed.

Love You, Aunt Zet

MAURICE HOLZENDORF, LOUISE'S BROTHER

I am a person who shows very little emotions. I hold a lot inside of me. I know this is bad. I have really found that out.

I have five wonderful sisters, and they all believe in God very strongly. When I was in Buffalo they were praying for me. I felt especially you, Louise. I know you prayed for me every day I had a bad problem with drinking. Like I said, I hold things in. I just don't like to reason things out. I called home every week to Mother. She told me what happened to you. It really killed me inside. I still didn't let my emotions out. I do remember the hurt I felt. I shed tears and stayed up just about all night visualizing and thinking, "Can't something else be done besides amputating?" I visualized how you look and said, "Oh my God, they are going to amputate her fingers and legs! There has got to be another way!" But knowing Louise, her belief in God and the will to live, what could I say? She's just too much. During that time I was still on the bottle and held my feelings inside. There had to be something I could do. I can see myself on the couch in Buffalo. But deep down, I knew that it was out of my hands. I did pray but I know God wouldn't accept my prayers because I was half high and had been that way for a long time. Thank God that I am now free from the bottle.

Louise's belief in God is just great. I know she knew God would take care of her. When I returned home and saw Louise, I did not show my emotions. But I said to myself, "OH, my goodness!" I felt it and I still do when I see her. I keep it inside because now I see how God has really taken care of you. I know one day I will have that close relationship with God. I know I'm the one who has to really accept not just speaking words deep down inside. I've been this way for thirty years. I didn't want to see her this way but God has taken care of Louise. It's wonderful seeing what Louise is doing. You are very independent, driving and doing many things. God has blessed you very much.

I also think back during the time when you were in the hospital why I didn't take a flight home. I don't know why I didn't. I feel guilty about that. Besides your mother, brothers and sisters, God also had Louise's husband Jon here to help her. Now that's a real man. He really stood by you.

Another thought comes to my mind. All of that praying Louise did for me when I was in Buffalo trying to get me straightened out and now Louise needs help and there is nothing I can do. That really hurts. Even today, I wish I could do something to help you. I know what you want; maybe some day. As I said before that it really killed me inside and I was helpless in Buffalo. There was nothing I could do but pray and thank God that Louise is alive, strong, and doing things that you wants to do in spite of her pain.

God bless you. I hope that Louise will be able to use a few of these words for her book. I love Louise and Joan loves her too.

Maurice Holzendorf, Brother

THE NIGHTMARE, BY ANNE BARGER (A FRIEND)

I met Louise, a beautiful lady, in 1979 when I was transferred into the school where she was teaching.

Over the ensuing years, we grew closer through our love for children and our love for God and I began to realize that she was beautiful inside as well as outside. We were more than friends. We were true sisters in Christ. In 1994, when Louise went into the hospital with pneumonia, it seemed as if someone had ripped off my right arm. When I found out that she would lose her fingers and her feet, I was overwhelmed with remorse. I knew, though, that Louise would be all right, because she is a believer and has God on her side. Throughout her hospitalization and recovery, she tried to maintain a positive attitude. I am sure that there were days when Louise wanted to give up, but she did not. She kept pressing on toward her calling. She touched many lives by the way she accepted her circumstances. She will receive her reward one day when we meet on the glory shore.

Anne Barger, a Friend

JOAN FUDGE – A FRIEND

Dear Louise:

When you went into the hospital with pneumonia, I was in the struggle to get my day care business started and didn't know you were in the hospital. It was March or April when Ann Barger told me of your body changes. I couldn't imagine why or how that happened.

Your condition emotionally and spiritually was more of a concern to me. I have been delighted at your stability and acceptance. You have been a witness for Jesus because you have such faith in God and Jesus.

Joan Fudge, a Friend

124

A LETTER FROM ANNE

I miss you more than words can express. I miss your smile and your kind words. You are in my thoughts and prayers daily. Please return to us quickly and fill our lives with your beautiful smile and thoughtful personality. Does that sound selfish? Maybe, but we really do miss you and care deeply that you are hurting and we can't do anything but pray and trust Jesus.

You would be amazed at the change that has come to Bayview. There is a warmth that has been missing for years. There is a closeness that only Christian friends can share. There is open talk of God and His goodness, prayers and their importance, even love. I don't know if this is evident to everyone or just to me. People come to me to talk about God and praying. This change did not come as a result of someone's promotion or encouragement. It has just evolved through the grace of God and the caring thoughts we all hold for you. I pray the change will remain; I just regret you had to get sick and experience so much pain for "it" to happen.

Your sister is a very nice person. She has been so thoughtful to talk to my mother and keep us informed of your progress. It is love, and not nosiness that motivates our interest.

Do not fret about the cards, etc. you are receiving, just enjoy them. I know how much they can do to cheer and encourage. I encourage everyone to write you, to send a card or note. Let them love you this way; YOU DESERVE IT and besides, it makes us happy to send them. Along with this letter, I am sending a couple of little gifts, reminders that you are loved and missed. I hope they will brighten your room and your days.

It would be wonderful if you were here to talk to face-to-face but I can't have everything. So I'll talk through a letter and pray that one day soon you will feel ready to have visitors. I want my mother to be one of your first visitors, though, because I think she can help you understand you are not alone.

God Bless You and Love Anne

REGINA PENN

Reading this book was really a blessing to me. Each time I read it, it caused my faith to increase and to remember to glorify and praise God in the midst of my trials.

Thank you for the opportunity to proof this book.

PRAYERS ANSWERED

As I think back about that day.
When I heard about my dear friend's illness,
I didn't know what to say
I've never known a person so sweet and dear.
To hear that she was in a coma,
I couldn't help but shed a tear
I prayed each day for her recovery.
My prayers were answered to my discovery
with God leading the way I had no doubt.
I knew that God would bring her out.
I knew with God as the head.
There was nothing to dread.

By Linda Crawford Peterson, a Friend

CHIRESSE AVALOS

While typing this book I had to declare war against the enemy. He tried to stop me in more ways than one. It has been over two years and finally we've DONE IT and the devil is still defeated. God knew the right time. It's funny how God allowed this book to be completed during the time of the attack on America. This book will minister to many.

Louise, the anointing on this book has given me a revelation of compassion in a great way. I rejoice constantly for the things we often take for granted, such as the breath we breathe, a peace of mind, the use of our limbs, and the list goes on...

I pray that your healing will manifest and that you continue to maintain peace as you have demonstrated throughout this book during those devastating moments. I must admit that both tears of joy, as well as tears of sadness came upon me as I read about your story.

Thank God for praying families and friends. I felt God's power all through this book as you totally surrendered to Him. Thank you for demonstrating victorious Christian living, for having the boldness and courage to share your testimony with others, and most of all for allowing me to be your typist.

Thank God for you, Louise!

God Bless You Always, Chiresse Avalos

Oh how great is thy goodness, which thou hast laid up for them that fear thee; which thou hast wrought for them that trust in thee before the sons of men!

(Psalm 31:19, KJV)

Oh, how great is your goodness to those who publicly declare that you will rescue them. For you have stored up great blessings for those who trust and reverence you.

(Psalm 31:19, TLB)

If ye be reproached for the names of Christ; happy are ye; for the Spirit of glory and of God resteth upon you: on their part he is evil spoken of, but on your part he is glorified.

(1 Peter 4:14, KJV)

Be happy if you are cursed and insulted for being a Christian for when that happens the Spirit of God will come upon you with great glory.

(1 Peter 4:14, TLB)

Yet if any man suffer as a Christian, let him not be ashamed, but let him glorify God on this behalf.

(1 Peter 4:16 , KJV)

But it is no shame to suffer for being a Christian. Praise God for the privilege of being in Christ's family and being called by his wonderful name!

(1 Peter 4:16, TLB)

Chapter Twenty-Five

Tips for Amputees

I have had to try many different things as an amputee to make my life more comfortable. As an amputee you long for your body to feel like what you remembered before the amputation. I have also told you earlier that amputee bodies feel as if the limb that was cut off is still there. This is good; however, we are reminded that something is different because of the constant burning sensations of where the limb was previously.

Here are a few tips given to me. Because I am a child of God, I know they are from his Spirit.

1. Learn scriptures of encouragement. Say them everyday. They will come to your mind during the hard times. Those times will come.

The Lord gives his people strength. The Lord blesses them with peace.
(Psalm 29:11, NIV)

The Lord will give strength unto his people; the Lord will bless his people with peace.
(Psalm 29:11, KJV)

2. Don't see yourself as an amputee. See yourself the way God sees you-WHOLE.

3. Tell yourself I'm going to walk or use my hands the way I used to with these prostheses, no matter which limb has been taken away from you. Again, I say, see yourself WHOLE. You will be doing things with the help of God that will amaze you and others.

4. Don't let ANYONE call your body parts stumps! This word is too negative and humiliating. God made us with fingers, arms and legs. That's what we should see. (I'm not denying the amputations; I'm seeing myself as God sees me.)

5. I have noticed if I stand or walk too long, blisters and abrasions appear on the front or back of my knees and legs (notice I did say legs). In the hospital the nurses kept my legs wet down with saline. I now mix my own solution of salt and water and it really works for me. The bad part of this is I have to stay off of my feet for a whole day (you notice I did say feet) while using the wet pads.

6. I try to stay in style with my dressing and shoes. Longer dresses work better for me and I purchase shoes with rubber soles and wedge heels. (Easy Spirit at Penney's). I am presently looking for boots that are flexible and will fit my feet.

7. I find that trouser socks are better than knee highs. They are thicker and I don't have to change them as often.

8. Don't let anyone tell you the pain that you are experiencing isn't real pain. They call it phantom pain. We know that it is real!!

9. I have found during the wintertime my liners get very cold during the night (liners fit inside the prostheses attached to my legs.)

   When I put them on in the morning it sends chills through my body. I have found that placing them on a heating pad at night keeps them nice and warm until the morning or when I'm up at night. I place the heating pad in a drawer next to my bed. No more chills in the morning! Praise God, we have enough to deal with. Why should it be cold liners?

10. Don't give up expecting a miracle. Look at that beautiful sky; God made it and EVERYTHING! He can do ANYTHING!

11. During the day take off your prostheses and massage your limbs. Use Aloe Vera lotion and vitamin E oil. I have to make myself do this because I like to ignore my prostheses. They have become a part of my body. This is good.

12. It means so much to have someone to tell what you are going through, and how you really feel without upsetting them. Find that family member or friend.

13. Don't feel defeated when you cry. Get it out and start thinking and doing things that make you fell good and useful.

14. Don't be afraid to ask why. You are human. Study the scriptures. God will give you peace.

15. If you are a driver and have had your right leg amputated, this information may be of interest to some of you. I find driving with my prostheses

foot on the gas works for me. My car is fitted with hand controls, although I use only the hand control brake. This gives me a feeling of normalcy when driving. Of course this is an individual decision. Some of you may not feel as secure as I am with your prostheses. I have been driving this way for more than seven years without a problem.

We live within the shadow of the Almighty, sheltered by the God who is above all gods.
This I declare, that he alone is my refuge, my place of safety; he is my God, and I am trusting him. For he rescues you from every trap, and protects you from the fatal plague. He will shield you with his wings! They will shelter you. His faithful promises are your armor. Now you don't need to be afraid of the dark any more, nor fear the dangers of the day; nor dread the plagues of darkness, nor disasters in the morning.
Though a thousand fall at my side, though ten thousand are dying around me, the evil will not touch me. I will not share it. For Jehovah is my refuge! I choose the God above all gods to shelter me. How then can evil overtake me or any plague come near? For he orders his angels to protect you whenever you go. They will steady you with their hands to keep you from stumbling against the rocks on the trail. You can safely meet a lion or step on poisonous snakes, yes, even trample them beneath your feet!
For the Lord says, "Because he loves me, I will rescue him;p I will make him great because he trusts in my name. When he calls on me I will answer; I will be with him in trouble, and rescue him and honor him. I wills atisfy him with a full life and give him my salvation."

(Psalm 91:1-16)

Printed in the United States
46546LVS00001B/205-363